Preacher in the Dark

STEPPING OUT OF THE SHADOWS AND INTO THE LIGHT

Michael Quinones

ISBN 979-8-89043-120-2 (paperback)
ISBN 979-8-89043-121-9 (digital)

Christian Faith Publishing
832 Park Avenue
Meadville, PA 16335
www.christianfaithpublishing.com

Printed in the United States of America

This book is dedicated to all the people that
believed in me and never gave up on me.
I also dedicate this book to all of those preachers and church
members that are trapped in what seems to be an impossible
situation to get out of. I know it seems as if it's all over for
you, but I can assure you that this is not the end, and your
story is not over. There is a way out, and his name is Jesus!
And last but not least, I want to dedicate this book to my Lord and
Savior, Jesus Christ! You are the very reason why I breathe. You
broke me free from my prisons of darkness and brought me into
your glorious light. There are not enough letters in the alphabet
for me to formulate a word that could describe how I feel for
you. I love you so much. You are my everything! Thank you!

Imagine

Imagine living life and feeling all of what God wants to do to you, for you, and through you. Imagine feeling that there is such a potential in you to live such a life of freedom. Imagine all that, but now imagine that and feel like there is a wall stopping you from going forward and achieving that life that you feel that is for you. Imagine all that in you and feeling chains holding you down to a life that you weren't called to, a life you were never designed for.

Light is needed

I always say that humans are just like flowers and plants. Light is such a necessity for sustaining life on this earth. Humans need the light of God to be able to live. The Word of God tells us that God is the Father of lights. He is light. He is the origination of light and the source of all the light in existence. Light is needed to do and to exist. Without light, there is only death. Nothing could survive. With light comes heat. Light itself does not have heat, but it does have entropy and energy. So subsequently, when light hits something, some of the energy will be absorbed and turned into heat (internal energy). When the light of God hits us, we absorb the energy and have heat. Dead things have no internal heat.

When you see a dead body, the internal body temperature of the cadaver drastically lowers. It lowers because there is no heat or energy in the body. That energy is the light of God. The same happens with our spirit man. God never intended for us to live in darkness. He never intended for us to live outside the light that is he. He wants us to live in the light of his glory so that we can experience life and experience it more abundantly. He desires for you to walk out of your shadowy grave, roll away the stone, and walk into the light.

Confusion

Upon reading this book, you will have questions answered. Questions like "How can God use someone in sin?" I'm sure many

Introduction

Large crowds, bright lights, flyers, and promotions all feed the life and ego of a preacher. For so long, that was the goal for me and many other preachers. Seeking God takes on a whole new meaning when the motives for seeking him change. Seeing many men and women of God being used by God mightily, performing miracles, signs, and wonders as they traveled throughout the world was such an awe-inspiring thing to witness.

Many see a preacher and see the glory with which God uses him or her. But many fail to know the story behind the glory. Many fail to know the hell they had to go through to be where they are and, unfortunately, the hell that many are still in. I learned this painful realization when it was my turn to be called into the ministry. To be used by God has a high price, a price I didn't know I had to pay.

Why this book?

Why did I write this book? I wrote this book because there are many colleagues in the ministry that find themselves living double lives and not knowing how to get out, desiring freedom and not knowing how to be free. As preachers, we know the written Word of God. We tell everyone how to be free but fail to apply what we preach to ourselves. Oftentimes, it is easy to walk people into the life of faith they should live but struggle secretly to have faith for ourselves.

Thanks and Appreciation

I want to thank my wife, Elizabeth, for showing me grace and mercy at a time when I needed it the most, for being a rock and constant in my life. When all have left me, you never left. You have been a compass to point me toward the faith to walk and ultimately reach the throne of God. Words will never be enough to say how thankful I am. I love you! I want to thank my pastor, Reverend Jose Rivera. I know him as Kenny. Thank you for never forsaking me. Thank you for never turning your back on me, even when you saw the worst in me. I want to thank you for showing me what a true man of God looks like, for teaching me the Word of our beloved Savior, Jesus Christ. I appreciate who you are. You have been more than a pastor. You have been like a father to me.

I want to give a special thanks to the church that graces me with the privilege to be called their pastor. I want to say thank you to Christ Saves Church! You are the reason why I do what I do. Since the birth and inception of CSC, I have strived to be the best servant to you. I truly am grateful for your love and for your devotion toward the Lord. I love you, and I pray that this book serves as one of the many weapons in the arsenal God has given us to fight this battle in the faith.

of us have asked this or have been asked this question. I don't blame anyone for asking such a question. It is not a crazy answer. We have been told by a pastor or a preacher that God does not use someone that is in sin or not right with God. But shocking scandals have shown us that it is the complete opposite. God can and does use people that are not right with him.

I am not saying that God condones being in sin and serving in the church. But I am saying that the God that we serve is not afraid of our sin and does not throw us away like trash when we fall short of the glory of God. He actually already knew your sin before you committed it and already devised a plan to deal with it. Walking in darkness and light for many ministers and Christians, unfortunately, is not as uncommon as you might think.

There are too many hidden things that God is uncovering in these last days, things that have caused a great deal of confusion within the church of Jesus Christ. But today, God chooses to reveal what has been covered for so long. Tactics the enemy of the souls has used for thousands of years against the crown of God's creation. God is penetrating the very core and shedding light on the inner workings of the kingdom of darkness. Gone are the days of the hidden truths within the body of Jesus Christ.

The body is sick

This book hopes to bring healing to the church. The apostle James shows us that healing comes out of confession. Unconfessed sin has a way to open the door to sickness, disease, and death. When confession is lived, the power of healing comes in and restores that which the enemy tried to destroy. The church body oftentimes experiences moments when viruses that infiltrate it. Like any virus, it needs to be identified to know how to treat it properly. That is exactly what God is doing. He is identifying what is wrong with the body of his Son.

When there is healing, we can see strength and confidence in those that serve. We can see how relationships can come out of the deepest and darkest of places. How resurrection isn't just something that we talk about once a year in the spring, you'll be able to experience the same power that rose Jesus out of the grave. We can live a life that screams freedom and life. That is what we were called to, a life that proclaims the name of Jesus, just by living. Our lives become sermons.

The desire has to be greater

This life that I speak of cannot be achieved simply because someone says you should have it. There has to be a drive and desire to be set free from what has us bound. There has to be a deep inner yearning for freedom. God has given us the power to be called the sons of God. He has given us the power and authority to choose what life we want. There is a freedom in Christ that has been predestined for you.

The apostle tells us to be free with the liberty that God has set us free with. That means it's a choice. We have to choose to be free. That choice is made when the desire to be free is stronger than the fear of being enslaved by sin. When your desire to be free is greater, God will meet you right where you are. He will run to you with the power of His Holy Spirit to set you free and wash you with the blood of Christ.

Who should read this book?

This book will walk you through and give you a window view of my personal journey and lead you into the light of freedom from the darkness in you that no one sees. Yes, I said it! You're living in darkness! This is a hard and very humbling realization. But I promise you that when you accept the truth in your life, you will feel the freedom that only the Holy Spirit can produce.

I also wrote this book for those people who are quick to destroy preachers that fall into sin, believers and nonbelievers alike. Yes, I agree that they are absolutely wrong for falling into sin. Preachers are morally held to a higher standard regarding holy living. But they are human, nonetheless. Part of my fear in writing this book was how it could be perceived. My intentions was never to give a pass for those who preach on the altar but to shed light on a reality far more common than we want to admit.

It is so easy and sometimes fitting for the church and the public to scold a preacher. But how hard it is to see past the sin and look at the *why* and the *what*. Why did that preacher fall? What led him or her down that road of compromise? Every preacher is a father or mother. Every preacher is a son or a daughter. Every preacher is a human, made in the express image of God, designed to be the mouthpiece of heaven for a world so desperately in need of a loving and forgiving God. Unfortunately, preachers know this but fail to feel it for themselves.

Who else is this book for? This book is for the congregant of a church that is confused over how God can use someone that is living a double life. Those church members that have listened to the preacher every Wednesday during the midweek Bible study and every worship service on a Sunday. Coming up and throughout my ministerial journey and climb, I would often ask myself, even enter into conversations with people on how it could be possible for such a holy God to use an actively sinful person with such power. This would baffle me and many others, even until this day.

Lastly, I wrote this book for the preacher that is living in secret darkness. I wrote this book for that man or woman who is screaming on the inside and begging God and the congregation they are preaching to do something. I know firsthand how it feels to be in a room with people who are hanging on to every word you say. I know what it is to be the vessel that God is using to destroy the yoke over the person you are praying for but struggling with the sin you committed the day before. I wrote this book to pull you out, preacher! I wrote this book to let you know that you're not alone.

Loneliness, guilt, and shame are not only emotions, they are spirits. Your battle is not a physical one. The outward appearance of your struggle is only a manifestation of what is happening on the inside. The late-night urges that feel impossible to overcome have a devastating effect on the anointing. I wrote this book to show you how to overcome. I pray in the Almighty name of Jesus Christ that upon reading this book, you find the freedom that you so desperately desire. I pray that you step out of the dark and into the light.

1

The Beginning

She looked at me as I sang before I delivered the message that night. I knew she wanted me. Her piercing and intense glances were enough to interfere with my connection with God as I performed before the congregation. Yes, you read that right, performed. I performed, rather than ministered. I got to a point in my life and ministry where I was no longer connected to God. I went to minister to cover myself, cover myself from being discovered for who I really was.

What was just looks turned into years of bondage. What was once an "innocent teenage struggle" had now turned into chains the devil used to keep me in a dark world of lust and now adultery. "How did I get here?" I asked myself as I stood before the congregation who penetrated my soul with their stares. To answer this question, I have to take you back to the beginning where it all started, back to a time where God and church was not the norm in me and my family's life.

How it all began

The year was 1989, the house was packed and loud. My mother and stepfather had people over. "Go upstairs, the adults are partying." That's what we were told by my mother. That word *partying* didn't mean what most understand it to mean. There were drugs, alcohol, and illegal activity was heavy in the house. It was late. I and all the children of the adults that were there were upstairs in me and my siblings' rooms. We played as any normal children would play.

Some of my cousins were present, as were some kids I had never met before.

Among them was a family friend's son. He was much older than the rest of us. The majority of the children that were present were around the same age as I was. I was a six-year-old child. This night, I was molested by this much older teen. From that moment, I was introduced to a world of lust and pornography. Thank God I never struggled with homosexuality. But many people that I have spoken to that have gone through what I went through would, later in life, struggle with homosexuality and lesbianism (I'll address this in a later chapter).

That night was the beginning of what would be decades of a silent dark hell that would grip my very heart. Throughout the course of my molestation at the hands of this trusted teen, I was shown pornography by this teenager, and it captivated my mind. My young mind was not ready and developed enough to process the images that were in those magazines. I truly thought it was normal. I had no idea Satan was setting me up and chaining me to a life of sin and bondage.

This experience, as traumatic as it was, is the reality of many people. It is not unique to race, creed, ethnicity, culture, and environment. There is a large number of people that have kept silent of experiences like mine. In fact, sadly enough, many have not survived such an ordeal. According to the Department of Health and Human Services (HHS), the US Department of Health and Human Services' Children's Bureau report *Child Maltreatment 2010* found that 9.2 percent of victimized children were sexually assaulted. Crimes Against Children Research Center shows that one in five girls and one in twenty boys is a victim of child sexual abuse. These numbers are so hard to read, but they reflect an unfortunate reality for so many.

Where were my protectors?

You see, that dark night in 1989 was just a symptom of a much greater underlying issue. Most likely, as you're reading this, you have asked yourself where my parents were. Where were the people who were supposed to protect me from such a horrible situation? They were there. They were in the same house I was in. That is what makes this so horrifying for any loving, responsible parent to read. I was molested in the same house my parents were in at the same time they were there.

How could they protect me when they were living such horrible lives? They were under demonic rule. Satan owned us. This is the reality of many people. This is why the Gospel is so powerful. The truth is without Jesus as your Lord and personal Savior, Satan and the kingdom of darkness has a legal right to be in your life. It takes a life in Christ to know the true freedom that comes when in relationship with him. My parents were lost and addicted, addicted to drugs, alcohol, and an ungodly lifestyle. Because of my mother's drug addiction, my siblings and I were forced to live with other family members. My father was not in my life, and I didn't really have an example of what a man looked like. My sister was in between living with my aunt and grandmother. My younger brother was sent to live with my grandfather in Puerto Rico. I was left to live with my grandmother.

When people live this lifestyle, the victims are not only themselves but also their children. Abuse and neglect is so common among children whose parents are addicted to drugs and alcohol. The desire of an addict is to find the next fix. They are on a desperate hunt to avoid and escape "getting sick" or going through withdrawal. In their pursuit of their selfish satisfaction, the children pay a devastating price. Usually, that price is the price of their innocence. Some have even died. I just want to thank God that although things happened, he was there all along, protecting me from greater damage. My protector was Jesus himself!

Time went on, and my life with porn and masturbation was an everyday struggle. There was not a day that I didn't satisfy the urges of my flesh. Imagine a six-year-old, seven-year-old, even eight-year-old wrestling with sexual thoughts, thoughts that even adults couldn't fully comprehend, let alone a child. This was my reality. I lost touch with reality. I lost sense of what was acceptable. I could not view women as people. I viewed them as sexual objects. Yes, they were people to me, but I only looked at them as objects to bring a man pleasure, never knowing that sex was not just a physical act. I wasn't aware that sex was tied with emotions. You see, the people in the movies would never display that. They never showed how the heart is attached to sex. How could I know? I was just a child.

Satanic traps

From that moment on, I would find pornography everywhere. I would go visit friends in their homes, and they would show me pornographic videos as is common among young curious children who so happen to stumble upon their parents' videos and magazines. No matter where I went, Satan had a trap! I could not escape it. I would literally walk in the street and see porn magazines on the ground. The Bible says in John 10:10, *"The thief does not come except to steal, and to kill, and to destroy. I have come that they may have life, and that they may have it more abundantly."*

Satan set a trap for me. I was hooked, and I did not know it. Satan's plan is to steal your future from you by enslaving you into a life of bondage through sin as early on as he can. He tries to kill your hope by tricking you to believe that there is no way out, then ultimately destroys your life by accepting this and diving further into this evil lifestyle.

John 8:44 says, "You belong to your father, the devil, and you want to carry out your father's desires. He was a murderer from the beginning, not holding to the truth, for there is no truth in him. When he lies, he speaks his native language, for he is a liar and the father of lies."

Jesus speaks of what Satan did since the beginning. He accuses him of being a murderer from the beginning. Truth was not found in him. This is the plan of the kingdom of darkness. Light is the only defense to this dark evil!

You were created for freedom

It is only by the grace of Jesus Christ and his divine intervention that we can be set free from the grasps of the enemy. You were created for freedom.

Galatians 5:1 says, "It is for freedom that Christ has set us free. Stand firm, then, and do not let yourselves be burdened again by a yoke of slavery."

You were created to be free, free from the bondage of sin. The devil knows this all too well. He sets traps as early on as he can through generational curses. He assigns what are called familiar spirits to each child when they are born. These spirits have been in the family bloodline for generations (I will speak on this in a later chapter).

Not knowing that I was created for this life of freedom held me back from all that God had predestined for me. I was always spoken to about God. I was always taught who God was, well, as good as my family could with the little knowledge they had of him. Once I learned about God, I was fascinated and intrigued by the thought of such a great being. It wasn't until 1999 that I would encounter God and accept his Son as my Lord and personal Savior.

God was in my life all of this time, and I did not know it. Since before that dreadful night in 1989, until the day I surrendered my life to him, God was working in my heart. You see, morality comes from God. No one has to tell a child what right and wrong is as it pertains to humanity. Who teaches a child how to scheme and craft a lie to avoid punishment? This is something that is naturally inside of each human. We all are born with, as I call it, a moral compass. Here Solomon charges Shimei of knowing naturally in his heart all the wrong he did.

First Kings 2:44 states, "The king also said to Shimei, "You know in your heart all the wrong you did to my father David. Now the Lord will repay you for your wrongdoing."

God was telling me what I was doing wrong. I didn't and couldn't understand it. This is the case with everyone in the world. We can feel the call to righteousness. Without being shown what true righteousness is and where it comes from, we will wrestle with a silent internal war deep within us. Paul speaks of this in Romans 7:15–20, and it says:

> I do not understand what I do. For what I want to do I do not do, but what I hate I do. And if I do what I do not want to do, I agree that the law is good. As it is, it is no longer I myself who do it, but it is sin living in me. For I know that good itself does not dwell in me, that is, in my sinful nature. [a] For I have the desire to do what is good, but I cannot carry it out. For I do not do the good I want to do, but the evil I do not want to do—this I keep on doing. Now if I do what I do not want to do, it is no longer I who do it, but it is sin living in me that does it.

This internal struggle was my life partner for ten years, a strong evil addiction to pornography and masturbation, a disgusting mind, eyes full of filth. I would remember waking up in the mornings and saying, "God, get me out of this. Take this from me." *Psalm 66:17–20 states:*

> I cried out to him with my mouth; his praise was on my tongue. If I had cherished sin in my heart, the Lord would not have listened; but God has surely listened and has heard my prayer. Praise be to God, who has not rejected my prayer or withheld his love from me!

I had a sincere heart as I begged God to take this sickness that lived in my heart. God hears the prayers of someone that truly has a repented heart. He listens and intervenes in the lives of those who call on God for sincere and genuine help. Many times, people want God's help only to be free of the mess they have gotten into but not wanting a true relationship with God.

Demonic connections

As time went on, I would encounter people that were dealing with the same issues and addicted to the same things as I was. I never understood how I would always be surrounded by people that were going through the same things I was. No matter where I went, I was always connected to people that would keep me in the vicious cycle of sin. Schools are a major place where Satan and his demonic spirits enslave children. The devil is even using teachers. There has been a rise in cases of teacher-student relationships.

I always encourage parents who come to the church I pastor to always pray for their children before they leave the home to attend school. There is an all-out attack on our children. Satan is after the future of this nation. He is looking to steal, kill, and destroy their future, before they even have a chance to set their feet on the ground. It is so important to teach your children to pray and to study the Word of God. The Bible tells us, *"Train up a child in the way he should go, And when he is old he will not depart from it"* (*Proverbs 22:6*).

The enemy of the souls is trying to permanently tattoo the filth of this world in the minds of the young and innocent. The connections you make in life are not coincidental. Who you meet along the way is not a just because happenstance. God allows people into our lives for a reason. Some people have come to be a blessing to your life. Other's came to be a hindrance and an obstacle. Nonetheless, they serve a purpose in your life. God will always receive the glory from all our situations and encounters. The Word of God so famously says in Romans 8:23 that *all things* would work together for our good. It didn't say that some things or some of the good things would work together. Now this statement is made when one is in Christ. In Christ, no crisis is wasted. All the people that come to your life bring things, and those things serve a purpose for the betterment and growth of your life in Jesus. And again, I say, "In Christ, no crisis is wasted." You are to show Christ in your crisis.

But what about those who are not in Christ? This is where the demonic connections take place. Those that live a life without Jesus live this life and walk this earth without the divine covering and protection of God. The enemy knows this full well. He will place people in your life that will push his evil agenda further into your heart. There's never a shortage of godlessness in the world. The saying is true, "Birds of a feather flock together." This is what happened at the Tower of Babel. They were working together, united in a common goal until they were divinely interrupted. The inability to communicate halted the work they were doing, thus making them to seek others that could speak their language. The devil will place in the life of someone who is enslaved in bondage, someone who can speak their language.

Demonic connections are made to strengthen a bond between you and people who are bound by demonic spirits. During such encounters, people will experience manipulation, abuse, degradation, and confusion. Oftentimes, demonic spirits, through these people, will manipulate you into thinking that you can't live life without them, only for the chance to inflict on you the pain they are silently feeling. Pain looks for an escape route. Usually, pain will mimic the actions that are done because it's the only way the person knows how to say they're hurt.

Most times, people suffer abuse in their company because many people, when they are molested and abused, tend to do to others what was done to them. As a pastor, I have had cases that were brought to me to deal with of sexual abuse of minors. More often, I have found that the accused offender was also at some point a victim themselves. I have often asked myself the same question, "Why couldn't they just speak up when it first happened? It most certainly would have avoided all of this." This is a vicious cycle. The time to be free is now!

Long-lasting effects

My true life was a secret. I could not say what was happening on the inside. The ridicule, embarrassment, guilt, and shame was all too real. I had to keep it quiet. But the quieter I kept it, the stronger the addiction grew in me. Not fully understanding the seriousness of my addiction and the long-lasting complex effects it would have on me, I cruised through life thinking that this was normal. I had uncles and cousins that normalized pornography, so there quite possibly couldn't be anything wrong with it. But every so often, I would feel such a guilt that would crash into me like a wave crashing onto the beach. It was unbearable.

The addiction took over me. I was a slave. I did whatever it demanded. It finally got to a point where it was not as easy to hide. What I'm about to say is so embarrassing to admit and difficult to say. At the age of fourteen, I found a stack of pornographic magazines in my grandparents' house. Wanting to look at the magazine, I left the house with it and walked up the street. As I walked, I passed a lady getting into her car. She saw what I had, and she yelled at me. I tried to run away from her. When I looked back, there was a man in a minivan, driving, staring at me. As I attempted to run across the street, he cut me off with his van. It was her husband. He jumped out and pinned me down. They were upset because as I walked passed their house, their children saw what I had in my hands. I would have been upset, too, if it were my child. It was disgusting and despicable. But it was the beginning of what was to be a life of slavery.

A godly setup

On August 29, 1999, I was sixteen years old. I was a very talented and intelligent young man. A normal teenager into sports, music as I played music. I played many instruments. I had good grades and applied myself in school as much as I could. I had as much involvement in extracurricular activities as I could without having much parental support. I would say, on the outside, I had a normal upbringing for an inner-city teen. Everything that came along with being a teenager in the city was not what is considered normal in a perfect world. But what else did I know? This is the case with most inner-city families, just like in any family, no matter where they might find themselves.

Up until that day, for a whole year, I felt a tug in my heart to seek the Lord. I didn't know much. I didn't know the first steps to seeking the Lord. I just knew what my grandfather in Puerto Rico would tell me when I would go to visit him.

I want to say that now looking back at everything I have been through, I am convinced that God was in my life all along. I didn't know it. I didn't understand so much that was happening at the time, but God was so involved in every detail of my life. God set up my life for my future victory. He set up my life so that through my freedom, I can present you victory. Romans 8:28–30 states:

> And we know that all things work together for good to those who love God, to those who are the called according to His purpose. For whom He foreknew, He also predestined to be conformed to the image of His Son, that He might be the firstborn among many brethren. Moreover whom He predestined, these He also called; whom He called, these He also justified; and whom He justified, these He also glorified.

My conversion and "the end of my struggle"

You see, every so often, my mother would send for my brother to come back from Puerto Rico. This time, it was for a longer period of time. He was now in school here in the US. He, like many children, met a friend. He became good friends with this classmate. My mother asked to meet the parents of this classmate of my brother. My mother and the mother of this student met and spoke over the phone. They developed a friendship. Little did we know that woman was a born-again believer of Jesus Christ. She was a Bible-believing, tongues-talking, fire-breathing type of Christian.

She began to share the Gospel to my mother, and one thing led to another. My mother accepts the Lord Jesus Christ as her Lord and Savior. My mother began to visit the church. Come to find out, the mother of my brother's classmate was the wife of the pastor of the church. Like most teenagers, I didn't want to go. I would visit the church from time to time with my mother. I liked what I heard from the pastor. He was an awesome teacher.

The things he would teach would really minister to me. I was so impacted by the teachings but never gave my heart to the Lord. I spent months without visiting, and one day, on August 29, 1999, I received a phone call. I heard my grandmother yell my name that there was someone on the phone. When I answered it, I heard this deep male voice say, "God bless you." I didn't remember who it was. He introduced himself as pastor. That was the lead pastor of the church. He said, "Listen, we have a three-day revival going on at the church, and today is the last day. Would you like to go?"

At the time, I didn't know why I said yes, but now I know that it was the Holy Spirit pushing me to go. But I said, "Sure, I'll go." What was wild is that my older cousins were there at my grandmother's house as well and wanted me to get high with them. I thank God for that call because that call saved and changed my life. Minutes after I hung up the phone, an old 1980s Ford Econoline with multiple colors and missing hubcaps pulled up. The driver beeped the horn, and I was so embarrassed.

At this point, my cousins were laughing at me as I walked up to the van. When I opened the door, it was Pastor Kenny. He smiled at me and stuck his hand out to shake my hand. At that point, the ridicule I was receiving from my cousins didn't matter. That smile that my pastor gave me was so powerful. There was so much freedom in it. I wanted that.

I wanted the freedom he had. I determined to myself that from that moment on, I was going to stick to this man because I knew he had the freedom I was looking for. That day, I walked into a small storefront church. The place was packed. The music and singing was loud, the people were jumping and singing. There was so much commotion going on that I was shocked at how rowdy the people were. But what caught me by surprise was that everyone had that same smile and joy that Kenny had. I knew I walked into the right place.

There was an invited guest preacher for that afternoon. He was from Venezuela. One of the ushers sat me at the front pew. The invited preacher began to share his testimony. He testified of how he came to Christ. He shared how God saved his life. All this time, as I was listening, my mind was being flooded with a ton of questions. At the end of his testimony, he asked, "Is there anyone here that wants to reconcile with God?" Well, being that I up until that point never accepted the Lord, I didn't know what to do. But he kept asking and asking. Every time he asked, my heart would beat faster and harder because I knew I needed Jesus.

As he asked again, I mustered the courage and began to walk to the altar. As I walked, he looked at me and asked if I wanted to reconcile. I couldn't speak. All of a sudden, my knees got weak, and I dropped to my knees and wept like I had never wept before. My heart's floodgates were opened, and I cried with a desire to be free. I felt Jesus entering into my heart. I felt when the Holy Spirit began to make a home in my heart. They walked me to the altar, and I knelt down. I felt someone grab me as I was on my knees. I heard this person say, "Thank you, Lord. Thank you, Lord!" It was Pastor Kenny. He prayed and then said to me in my ear, "From this moment on, God will be your Father and everything you will ever need."

I took that to mean that my struggle was over. I felt like a brand-new man. I literally felt like the weight of the world was lifted off my shoulders. I felt so light. I could truly smile for the first time I could remember. I didn't have to fake the joy I felt. I was instantly in love with God. I was set free of everything! Or so I thought. I thought that my life was going to be perfect from that moment on as do so many new converts to Christ think.

I, at the time, like many Christians, naively believe that all of life's problems go away at the moment of conversion. But, sadly enough, that is not so. Many Christians, even ministers, believe that if you get it right at the altar, it's done. How wrong we are to believe such a lie. Many believe that prayer fixes everything. I'm sorry to burst your bubble, but unfortunately, there are some things you have to do. Now before I continue, let me start by saying that salvation is not about works as Paul says in Ephesians 2:8–9, *"For it is by grace you have been saved, through faith—and this is not from yourselves, it is the gift of God—not by works, so that no one can boast."*

What I didn't know at the time is that sanctification is a process. Holiness is done by God, and consecration is done by us.

I had to enter into partnership with God. I had to enter into agreement about my lifestyle change. Transformation doesn't just happen. The word *transformation* comes from the Greek word *metamorphoó, which means properly transformed after being with while keeping inner reality.* To be transformed is to move from one form to another. For transformation to take place in your life, you have to allow God to move you from where you are to where God wants to take you. Everything in our lives change when Jesus enters the heart.

A lifelong process

Sanctification is a lifelong process. I hope that while reading this book, you understand that trips, slips, and mess-ups were already calculated by God. Jesus died for your past, present, and future sins. He knew you would fall but died anyway! I, like many, had to divorce the thought of having to work for my sanctification. My call is to be obedient and to love God with all my heart, and his grace will work wonders. It would take me years to truly understand the concept of grace. I want to say that I am still learning each day about the glorious grace of Jesus Christ.

2

Familiar Spirits and Generational Curses

This is a war! Many tend to forget that we are at war with an unseen adversary. Our enemy is very astute when it comes to humans, especially the church. We are caught in a war that we didn't ask for. What did I do to make Satan so angry with me? What did you do to make the kingdom of darkness so adamant on destroying you? I can't think of anything, except for one thing: accepting Jesus Christ as my Lord and Savior.

Walking out of darkness and into the light of Christ is an all-out declaration of war against the kingdom of darkness. One of the devil's tactics is to keep you in the dark and away from the light of Christ. That light is the Word of God.

Landmines and sabotage

The Bible says in John 1:1–5 (NIV):

> In the beginning was the Word, and the Word was with God, and the Word was God. He was with God in the beginning. Through him all things were made; without him nothing was made that has been made. In him was life, and that life was the light of all mankind. The light

shines in the darkness, and the darkness has not overcome it.

The devil does not have the power to know the future, but he can see angelic and heavenly activity around a person. He is also aware of prophecies spoken over people. If you remember what he did throughout the Bible as he anticipated the arrival of liberators in the Bible, he attempted to kill even babies, all to stop the move of God among his people.

Exodus chapters 1 and 2 recount the story of the killings of the male children born of the Israelites. The new Pharaoh did not know Joseph and what was said by the previous Pharaoh. He looked and saw that the Hebrew people grew in number. He saw that they were greater than his own people. He devised a plan to stop their growth and to provide protection from future attacks by them. The plan was to tell the Hebrew midwives to kill any male child that was born. If it was a female, they were to let them live. When the midwives did not obey the command given by the king, he ordered for all of his people to cast every male that was born to the Israelites into the Nile River.

That was the earthly reason and explanation for this atrocity. But in reality, there was a true motive for this. This evil plan was not concocted in the mind of a human. It came from the spiritual realm. It came from Satan himself. You see, in Genesis 15:13, God tells Abraham (whose name was still Abram) that his people or seed would be a stranger in a land that is not theirs, and they would serve them; and they would afflict them for four hundred years.

At the time that the new Pharaoh made the Hebrew people slaves and attempted to kill the male children, more than four hundred years have passed. In Genesis 3:15, God gave the first prophecy concerning the Messiah. He told Satan that the seed of the woman would crush the head of the serpent. The seed is the offspring. Satan knew that the liberation of God's people would come from a male child born unto a woman of God's people. He spoke to Abraham about his seed. Satan heard the promise to Abraham. He heard four hundred years and was watching attentively the Hebrew people. The time has come. He was trying to stop what was going to happen.

He was attempting to kill off the liberator that would come to free God's people. This same thing happened during the time of Jesus's birth. Herod the Great, king of Judea, ordered the murder of all male children, two years old and younger, because of the prophecy of the coming king of Israel that would liberate his people. Satan's tactics do not change. He is actively trying to kill off the descendants of God's people. He is setting landmines and trying to sabotage your children to disrupt and destroy their future!

One of the plans of the devil is to attach familiar spirits onto a newborn child. These spirits have the charge to attach themselves to people, learn and study the person. Also, they travel through the bloodline and live in the family for generations. These are called generational curses (I will speak on this further in the chapter). The Word of God speaks of these types of spirits. I'm going to give you some verses to show you how these spirits operate. It is important to note that I reference the NIV for the verses. The NIV uses the word *mediums*, whereas the King James uses familiar spirits. They are one and the same.

"Do not turn to mediums or seek out spiritists, for you will be defiled by them. I am the Lord your God" (Leviticus 19:31 NIV).

"The Egyptians will lose heart, and I will bring their plans to nothing; they will consult the idols and the spirits of the dead, the mediums and the spiritists" (Isaiah 19:3 NIV).

Acts 16:16–18 (NIV) states:

> Once when we were going to the place of prayer, we were met by a female slave who had a spirit by which she predicted the future. She earned a great deal of money for her owners by fortune-telling. She followed Paul and the rest of us, shouting, "These men are servants of the Most High God, who are telling you the way to be saved." She kept this up for many days. Finally Paul became so annoyed that he turned around and said to the spirit, "In the name of

Jesus Christ I command you to come out of her!"
At that moment the spirit left her.

You see, these spirits speak as if they are past family members. They have been in the family bloodline for generations. They are the ones that introduce the past destructive behaviors of your family to you. They travel after the death of a family member, on to the next person. They increase in power and authority as long as there is no liberator. The longer they dwell and live among the generation, the more ownership they claim of the people and family. This is part of the landmines the devil lays in people's lives.

Now I'm going to say something that many will not agree with, and many will even be very upset with what I'm going to say, but many preachers, ministers, and clergymen are preaching and serving in churches while having these spirits in their lives. I am a witness and also am writing to you as a survivor of this. I have had numerous conversations with ministers that would tell me that they were actively in sexual sin or addicted to pornography while in ministry. This is far too common among the church of Jesus Christ.

Guilty preaching

Ministry to many is a badge of honor. It is an accolade for so many. When I was coming up in the church and ministry, I would see how these men and women of God would minister and be used by God. The way they would be used in the gifts was so amazing to witness. But what I didn't know was the struggle that many were dealing with as they traveled and preached the Word of God. On the outside, it was glorious. It was so powerful, the display of God's manifestation. But what I did not see was the internal struggle and hell that many lived and unfortunately still live. I know this firsthand. I am a living witness to this struggle.

I remember, many times, I would get the call and be invited to minister the Word of God at a church in either my local city or abroad and be excited to preach. I would prepare my messages for the churches. I would pray as much as I could. But I would still battle with pornography and lust. I would still have lustful eyes for women; and that was the heart that I would go with and preach the Gospel.

Countless times, I would get to the church and pray before I would go up to the pulpit, "God, please forgive me. Please don't punish these people for what I did. They deserve to hear your Word." Or I would beg God to not expose me on the altar. I would tell God that if he forgave me one more time, I would stop the porn, masturbation, and lust. I would preach, the Holy Spirit would speak and move with power, but my conscience and the Holy Spirit would be convicting me as I preached.

I would preach with such guilt. It was so hard to ignore the voice of the Holy Spirit deep inside my soul as I preached. My sin was a constant reminder of the hypocrisy I was living. Here I am telling people to be free when I myself was bound by the very thing I was pretending to have overcome. This reality is far more common than you would think in the lives of so many ministers. This, what I'm talking about, is taboo in the ministerial community. This is what is not spoken. This is what the devil does not want you to know.

Satan is cursing the bloodline of many preachers. There are many ministers that are second, third, and even fourth-generation preachers. But in those generations, there are satanic curses that have not been broken. The struggles that are secretly dealt with need to be broken for true breakthrough.

Sins of the father

There is a chapter in the Bible that many people read and just pass over as just a historical chapter. But when you truly take an in-depth look, you'll see how there were curses that traveled through the generations until the liberator showed up. In Matthew, chapter 1, we read about the generations that were before Jesus. In the beginning of the chapter, it says, "*The book of the* generation of Jesus Christ, the son of David, the son of Abraham." Let's take a closer look at what was happening throughout the generations.

Verse 2 starts off by saying, "Abraham was the father of Isaac, Isaac the father of Jacob, Jacob the father of Judah," and so forth.

Let's just focus on the first three. Who was Abraham? Abraham was a man from the land of Ur (the Babylon region in Mesopotamia). He was married to a woman named Sarah. When you read the account of Genesis 12:10, you see how Abraham (at the time was named Abram) goes to Egypt due to the famine in the Negev where he was.

When he gets there, he tells his wife, Sarah (whose name was Sarai), to say that she was his sister, rather his wife on account of her being so beautiful. He feared that they would kill him and keep her. Here you can see the spirit of fear operating in Abraham that convinced him to lie. Now this would not be the only time Abraham did this. In Genesis 20:11–12, Abraham has now moved to the region of the Negev and lived between Kadesh and Shut. The Bible says that for a while he stayed in Gerar. In Gerar, Abraham meets Abimelech, the king of Gerar. Abraham tells the king Abimelech that Sarah was his sister.

After the meeting between Abraham and Abimelech, God speaks to Abimelech in a dream. He tells him that he was as good as a dead man because he took Sarah for himself. God tells the king that she was a married woman and that her husband was a prophet. Abimelech pleads with God because he did the thing with clean hands and a clear conscience. God tells him that he spared him and did not let him touch Sarah. Once confronted, Abraham was questioned why he did such a thing.

He tells the king the same thing he says in chapter 12. He was afraid that because there was no fear of God in the land, that they would kill him and take his wife. You see how the sin repeats itself? The spirit of fear was accompanied by a lying spirit in a moment where a false reality was presented. Abraham opened the door to this curse due to his lack of faith in what the Lord had promised him. This was a curse that Abraham would pass on to his son, Isaac.

The story repeats itself. Isaac is now in the same situation that his father, Abraham, was. There was a famine. He was told by the Lord to go to Egypt for an allotted time by the Lord. From there, he went to Gerar, just as his father did. He met Abimelech and was now visited by that same spirit of fear. Coincidence? I think not! In fact, I am 100 percent sure it's not. The struggles and sins of his father were now his reality. He feared that they would see his wife, Rebekah, kill him and take her for their own. One day, the king looks down from his window and sees Isaac caressing his wife, Rebekah. This is a curse that traveled through the bloodline. Now the blood is not cursed, but these spirits have attached themselves to the family.

Isaac has two sons named Esau and Jacob. Many times, in the Bible, the names given to the children are very significant and important. The name Esau means handling rough for he was to be a wild man. Jacob means heel catcher and supplanter for he was born holding onto the heel of his brother, Esau, and later would steal and supplant his brother's blessing. He lied and took advantage of the poor eyesight of his father, Isaac. The same sin is now presenting itself. Do you see a pattern here?

Half-truths and justification

Abraham told a half lie. He told enough truth to cover himself and to justify himself in the event of being caught. Or so he thought. This situation is what plagues many preachers. Countless times, I found myself convincing myself that I was okay because of X, Y, Z. But the truth was and still is that a half lie is equal to a whole lie. Jesus is the truth. God didn't send half of the truth to the world. So we as carriers of the truth must present the entire truth of God. The truth can never be cut in half. We are to present all of ourselves as living sacrifices to God. *"Therefore, I urge you, brothers and sisters, in view of God's mercy, to offer your bodies as a living sacrifice, holy and pleasing to God—this is your true and proper worship"* (*Romans 12:1 NIV*).

God is patient

Throughout the entire first chapter of the Gospel of Matthew, we see sin all throughout the generations. Bear in mind that these were the people that were in the bloodline of Jesus. Notice that although there was sin in the bloodline, God continued to deal with them. You see, the glory of God is displayed in his grace and mercy throughout this genealogy. Although Abraham lied, God was merciful and faithful. God understood that Abraham had faith but still had a struggle. God knew that Satan was trying to derail the plan of God. This is what happens in the lives of many ministers. God has a plan and a purpose with a preacher, but he knows that they still have struggles.

The light shines in darkness

Part of what keeps the curse alive in many people is keeping the curse hidden in darkness. This is one of the most effective tools the enemy has to keep people in bondage. By not shining a light to what is in the dark or better known as confessing, the enemy can continue to stay in your life hidden and undetected. Satan and his cohorts move in darkness. They would love to never be discovered. This is why they do whatever they can to not allow people to know the Word of God. The Word of God is light. In the book of Psalms, it states, *"Your word is a lamp for my feet, a light on my path"* (*Psalm 119:105 NIV*).

Jesus tells Nicodemus in the Gospel of John, chapter 3, verse 20, *"Everyone who does evil hates the light, and will not come into the light for fear that their deeds will be exposed."* This is a perfect example of what happens. There are numerous preachers that are living with hidden sin and struggles but dread to speak up to be free for fear of being exposed and losing what they have. I lived like this for many years. This was one of the hardest things I ever had to deal with. I was trapped, and no one knew. Or at least that's what I thought. The danger of living and preaching like this is found in the Gospel of *Matthew 7:21–23* (*NIV*), and it says:

> Not everyone who says to me, "Lord, Lord, will enter the kingdom of heaven, but only the one who does the will of my Father who is in heaven. Many will say to me on that day, "Lord, Lord, did we not prophesy in your name and in your name drive out demons and in your name perform many miracles? Then I will tell them

plainly, 'I never knew you. Away from me, you evildoers!'"

There is a terrible day known as judgment day. This day struck fear in the heart of the apostle Paul. Second Corinthians 5:10–11 states:

> For we must all appear before the judgment seat of Christ, so that each of us may receive what is due us for the things done while in the body, whether good or bad. Since, then, we know what it is to fear the Lord, we try to persuade others. What we are is plain to God, and I hope it is also plain to your conscience.

It is truly dangerous because we will all stand before the throne of God to give an account for everything we have done in this body and life. We will stand in judgment before an Almighty, righteous, and just God. This is what has kept me up at night for many nights. I was living a lifestyle that was contrary to what God stipulated in his Word. James 4:17 says, *"If anyone, then, knows the good they ought to do and doesn't do it, it is sin for them."* The dangerous part is that a preacher knows the truth. But this isn't just for the preacher. This is for everyone who calls themselves Christians. In fact, anyone who has ever been in contact with the Word of God. There is no excuse that could ever be valid before the Lord. It is time to shed light on the darkness living on the inside!

The curse has to break

God's desire is for everyone to be free. He doesn't just stand idly by, watching the suffering of his creation that desperately desires to be free. God listens to the cries of his people. He made us to be free from a life of sin and bondage. In Exodus 3, he speaks to Moses and tells Moses that he has heard the cries of his people.

> The Lord said, "I have indeed seen the misery of my people in Egypt. I have heard them crying out because of their slave drivers, and I am concerned about their suffering. So I have come down to rescue them from the hand of the Egyptians and to bring them up out of that land into a good and spacious land, a land flowing with milk and honey—the home of the Canaanites, Hittites, Amorites, Perizzites, Hivites and Jebusites." (Exodus 3:7–8 NIV)

God hears the cry of someone who wants to be free. How many times have you prayed the same prayer from a place of shame and guilt, saying, "God, forgive me. I have sinned again in the same sin. Help me"? I had done this more times than I could count. I have begged God to set me free of the masturbation, pornography, lust, and sexual thoughts. I would pray this on the altar as I got ready to expound my message. Many times, I would beg God to take it from me. But he never did. At one point, I stopped asking because I thought there was no hope for me.

But, my goodness, the grace and mercy never stopped flowing. Every single time, God would touch me. He would whisper his love to me. He would shower me with his presence, and I couldn't understand how such a wretched soul that I was could be touched by such a Holy God. You see, God waits patiently for the desperation to reach the heart of a person. It is only in that desperation that one reaches rock bottom, where they are truly tired of the sin. It wasn't that God didn't want to take it from me or that he didn't want to help me. It was that he was letting me get tired of my sin.

When you're truly tired, there is a prayer of desperation that comes out of your soul. That's when God shows up. Do you remember the demoniac? Do you remember how he made his home among the tombs? How he would hurt himself and cut himself with stones? He would cry day and night. It seemed as if his days and nights of crying among the tombs went unnoticed. Or that he was just throwing words in the air. But God was listening. It was no coincidence that Jesus landed at the shores of Gadara.

Jesus deliberately came ashore to where the need was. The demoniac's cries were what made Jesus come to him that fateful day. The cries of desperation are what turns the face of the Father to us. There needs to be desperation and a genuine desire to be free. Jesus is the curse-breaker. In Matthew, chapter 1, Jesus broke the curse. He changed the course of sin in the bloodline. When Jesus comes, the curse of sin and death is truly broken. He chose you to break the generational curse in your life and family. Are you tired yet? Are you truly desiring to be free? Today is the day to be set free of the curse.

3

Sin Has an Objective, and Your Flesh Has an Appetite!

The phone call not only startled me, but it also impressed me. I was a few months into serving the Lord and going to church faithfully, but I was still bound to porn and masturbation, dealing with lust at a fierce level. I was doing what was the norm in the church, and I did not know it. I started to connect with my peers in the church, teens whose parents were prominent in the church and other churches. I thought that they were so spiritual and godly. That's what you would expect, coming from such a godless lifestyle. You viewed all Christians as holy and righteous.

But soon enough, I found out that wasn't the truth in most cases. I was actually confronted with the reality that Christians struggled with sin as well. Heck, some Christians even actually lived worse lifestyles than nonbelievers. I was in church and loved God. I truly fell in love with God. He was so real in my life. He was so powerfully present in my life, but I was still struggling with lust, still bound by pornography and masturbation. Sin is progressive. It never just stays at its beginning stage. It is a cancer that grows on the inside, and if not dealt with, consumes the very life of a person, both spiritually and physically.

The call

It was now four months into my conversion, and I was soaking everything up like a sponge. I grew in knowledge of the Lord and got deeper in the church. I was always praying and seeking the Lord. I fell head over heels with God. You couldn't keep me away from the house of God. All I wanted to do was to be in a church service. It was my escape from the world. I was in awe of God. I was actually growing in knowledge and love for God and his Word. But, unfortunately, there was something else growing within me as well. It was my lust. My lust was starting to grow right along with my knowledge and love for the Word. I was still dealing with masturbation and watching porn and going to church. I didn't know how to get rid of it. The more I learned the Word of God, the more convicted I felt. But still no answer on how to stop.

The church I was a member of was old-school Pentecostal, so we had church four times a week—Monday, Wednesday, Saturday, and Sunday. I loved it. One Tuesday night, I was home after working a part-time job. I got a phone call from the worship leader of the church who was also an evangelist. He was a powerful man of God (I'll talk about him later in the book). I answered the phone, he asked me how I was doing, and of course I told him I was doing fine. He then told me that he had to tell me about a dream that he had.

At this point, I was well aware that God revealed things through dreams. So I was paying attention to what he was about to say. So he then began to tell me that in his dream, he saw me in my room and that I began to masturbate. He said that he didn't see in detail but that he could see me doing that. He felt in his dream that I was actively doing that. He then told me that God was watching me, that I didn't need to do that, that God wanted to free me of that. Of course, I was embarrassed but pleased at the same time because it meant that God was watching and listening to me. The phone call not only startled me, but it impressed me. I admitted that I was engaging in that. He prayed with me and did not shame me. He didn't make me feel guilty but led me to my brief freedom. I literally stopped masturbating and the consumption of porn. The next eight months were amazing. I was actually free!

Temptation

The Bible is so powerful and accurate. How could these men, thousands of years ago, speak on things that would be happening today with such accuracy? How could they know in such detail about the dealings of the hearts of today? It is now eight months later, Saturday morning, and I was home alone. I was watching television, and I felt a nudge to pray. I kept ignoring it because I wanted to just do nothing that Saturday. All of a sudden, I started to think on the pornography that I watched in the past. I started to feel tempted to watch porn.

As you are reading this, you're identifying with what I am saying. How many times have you felt the impulse to pray or read your Bible, and you just go on about your business as if you felt nothing? That feeling is the Holy Spirit telling you that God wants communion with you. The Bible says in Romans that the Spirit takes on our infirmity. *"In the same way, the Spirit helps us in our weakness. We do not know what we ought to pray for, but the Spirit himself intercedes for us through wordless groans"* (Romans 8:26 NIV).

Him taking on your infirmity is done when you pray. He partners with you in your prayer. He carries the weight from your issue and intercedes for you. The Bible says that he does so with wordless groans. Those are the words that you cannot utter that you would like to express. He sees your weakness in a matter and preemptively attempts to commune with you to strengthen you before the temptation comes knocking at your door.

It is in those preemptive prayers that he equips you with the way out of the temptation that comes to push you to fall into sin that God freed you from.

"No temptation has overtaken you except what is common to mankind. And God is faithful; he will not let you be tempted beyond what you can bear. But when you are tempted, he will also provide a way out so that you can endure it" (1 Corinthians 10:13 NIV).

Here I sat with the decision to pray, and I just ignored the still small voice of the Holy Spirit. Temptation came, and I fell. I went right back into the sin that God took me out of. I felt so ashamed. I felt so sad and defeated. Freedom is to be lived in. Freedom is to be cherished because freedom isn't free. It costs the blood of the Son of God. It costs the Father the best that he had. He gave his one and only Son for you to be free.

"So if the Son sets you free, you will be free indeed" (*John 8:36 NIV*).

Downhill fall

I began to spiral out of control. The shame and guilt that I felt was so strong that it kept me from praying. This is often the case when someone falls from grace and into sin. These are not only feelings and emotions, but they are also demonic spirits. These two spirits and emotions are designed to keep you out of the presence of the Lord. They fight to keep you from praying because prayer is vision and connection. Their first appearance was in the garden of Eden. Adam and Eve had just bitten into the fruit of the tree of good and evil. Their eyes were opened, and they knew they were naked. Prior to their eyes being opened, they were in a perpetual state of innocence. They did not know that they were naked. They only knew a relationship with God.

The Bible says that God came into the garden in the cool of the day. The word *cool* here comes from the Hebrew word *ruach*, which means spirit or wind. The word *day* comes from the Hebrew word *yom*, which means "appointed time in the day." So essentially, what it is saying is that his Spirit would come in at a specific time in the day. So Adam knew that God would come to visit him at a certain time in the day, but he hid because of the sin that was committed.

Adam committing sin caused him to feel guilt and shame. The guilt and shame stopped him from getting to the meeting place with God. This is what is happening to many preachers and Christians. A fall from grace is not an easy thing to deal with. But the aftereffects are even far more difficult to face.

The order of a fall—2 Corinthians 10:4–5 / James 1:14–15

Stronghold: that area in your flesh and mind that has not been defeated. The enemy will launch his attack from that place in your flesh and mind.

Thoughts/imaginations/arguments: voices that sound and are disguised as your own thoughts that exalt itself against the knowledge of God.

Luring: using your fleshly desire to entice you.

Consummation of the desire: to produce a seed of death.

This is how the enemy operates. The serpent knew that Adam and Eve were naturally attracted to the tree and its fruit, which is why he used it. Satan doesn't need an entire arsenal of weapons to fight you. All he needs is for you to be attracted to what God does not want for you. The apostle James says it like this:

> When tempted, no one should say, "God is tempting me." For God cannot be tempted by evil, nor does he tempt anyone; but each person is tempted when they are dragged away by their own evil desire and enticed. Then, after desire has conceived, it gives birth to sin; and sin, when it is full-grown, gives birth to death. (James 1:13–15 NIV)

James and the self-righteous Jews

Countless times, I have thought to myself, *I prayed and because I prayed, I am good now. I am doing well.* We are not to rely on our own strength. We are to always rely on Jesus. The strength and help from his Holy Spirit in our lives is what we ought to seek after. This is what James the apostle had to address in his epistle. He had to speak to the twelve tribes of Israel and tell them what the truth was. You see, just like the apostle Paul, James had to deal with the self-righteousness in the lives of the Jews. Because they were Jewish, they thought that they had this down already, so he had to remind them that they had to put their faith to work.

"What good is it, my brothers and sisters, if someone claims to have faith but has no deeds? Can such faith save them?" (James 2:14 NIV).

James knew that they wanted to sit back and just boast on the fact that they were good now because they accepted Jesus Christ as their Messiah. It is not enough to just pray. There has to be some steps filled with faith involved here. This starts with humbling yourself.

"Humble yourselves before the Lord, and he will lift you up" (James 4:10 NIV).

Humbling oneself is how God begins to lift you out of the pit of despair. This is what it takes. Just like the Jews, many preachers and even church members are, sad to say, not humble. Humility takes us from knowing it all and being autonomous to total dependency on God. This is what is truly missing in today's church. We are living in the age of the influencer. We no longer have preachers and ministers. We now have influencers. Being a minister today means that you have to have a certain level of followers, be very popular, have the best flyers, have the best photos, have to constantly post photos/videos of yourself ministering and many selfies with a scripture to justify it.

This is so sad. Many times, when preachers seek after all the attention and popularity, it is a sure sign that there is something happening behind closed doors. You might say that this is not true. But let's look at this a little closer. Because the church body is somehow convinced that to be successful in ministry, you have to be big on social media. Many ministers spend a considerable amount of time on these platforms. Let's look at how long the average person consumes social media. A study on social media usage was conducted, and they found that the average daily usage is the following:

> Facebook: thirty-three minutes
> YouTube: nineteen minutes
> Instagram: twenty-nine minutes
> WhatsApp: twenty-eight minutes
> Twitter: thirty-one minutes

Snapchat: thirty-one minutes
LinkedIn: one minute
Pinterest: 14.2 minutes
TikTok: thirty-two minutes

This adds up to over three hours of consumption a day, 3.63 hours a day to be exact. Now you might say that's not a lot of time. But consider this, most preachers and Christians do not live in full-time ministry. The majority of minsters are bivocational. Most ministries cannot afford to pay the salary of a minister as church attendance today is at an all-time low due to the recent pandemic. The money isn't there as it used to be.

Question is, where do they get the time to pray? If all the time is spent on work, social media preparation, photoshoots, promotions, and flyers, where do you find the time to pray, read the Bible, fast, and get deep with the Lord? This is a satanic plan to keep the ministerial body occupied on what is not important. Now I'm not totally against social media. I do believe that we have to be in that platform as well. Today's generation is there, and we have to be where they are. But we should not be consumed and caught up with it. Just as the three Hebrew boys in the book of Daniel. They were in Babylon but chose to not be contaminated and bow down to the culture. The Word of God puts it this way:

"Do not conform to the pattern of this world, but be transformed by the renewing of your mind. Then you will be able to test and approve what God's will is—his good, pleasing and perfect will" (*Romans 12:2 NIV*).

To conform means to take the shape of something. We are in the world but not of it. We are to move from form to form until we reach the form of the Lord Jesus Christ by renewing our minds. This is done by putting on the mind of Christ as Paul states. Doing this will prove his good, pleasing, and perfect will in our lives.

Sin's objective

From the moment that Adam and Eve fell, sin has been present in the life of humanity. The book of Genesis explains this. Moses, as he wrote this, gives God's take on the matter. He perfectly lets us know what sin's objective in the life of a person is. When God spoke to Cain, he tells him that sin was crouching at his door. Now this is so powerful and telling because God was being so honest with Cain, and Cain's stubbornness would not allow him to see what was happening around him.

God was telling him that sin was crouching. This is the Hebrew word *rabas*. It means to crouch on all four legs, like a recumbent animal. This is describing a sneaky prowling animal, almost lying flat, ready for an attack. The door was his heart. God was telling him that sin was lurking, and its desire was to destroy him. We can see this in Revelation 3:20, "*Here I am! I stand at the door and knock. If anyone hears my voice and opens the door, I will come in and eat with that person, and they with me.*"

Your flesh is hungry

In the same way that sin was personified, the flesh is given human attributes as if it's a separate entity from us. The flesh has desires and an appetite. Paul addresses this in Galatians chapter 5. He explains that the flesh has a desire. The flesh is looking to be satisfied.

"*For the flesh desires what is contrary to the Spirit, and the Spirit what is contrary to the flesh. They are in conflict with each other, so that you are not to do whatever you want*" (Galatians 5:17 NIV).

Your flesh is hungry. It is hungry for the things of this world. Who is being fed? Your spirit or your flesh? This is the issue that we are facing. We have a generation of preachers and church members that are being fed so much of the world that the world has become homogeneous with the church. This should not be. Paul addresses this while addressing the church in Corinth in his second letter to them.

Do not be yoked together with unbelievers. For what do righteousness and wickedness have in common? Or what fellowship can light have with darkness? What harmony is there between Christ and Belial? Or what does a believer have in common with an unbeliever? What agreement is there between the temple of God and idols? For we are the temple of the living God. As God has said: "I will live with them and walk among them, and I will be their God, and they will be my people." Therefore, "Come out from them and be separate, says the Lord. Touch no unclean thing, and I will receive you." And, "I will be a Father to you, and you will be my sons and daughters, says the Lord Almighty." (2 Corinthians 6:14–18 NIV)

We have to go back to eating the spiritual food that God provides his people. This issue is not new at all, really. The children of Israel dealt with the same issue in the wilderness. They left Egypt, following Moses. They desired food and meat. But, instead, God gave them fresh manna from heaven. This food came directly from heaven. This could not be found anywhere here on earth. They were being fed by God himself. It not only fed them physically, but it was spiritual nourishment. Psalm 78 describes the plight the Israelites had with having to leave the food they had in Egypt. Asaph recounts the story but in verses 24–25, he says specifically that manna was angels' food.

"He rained down manna for the people to eat, he gave them the grain of heaven. Human beings ate the bread of angels; he sent them all the food they could eat" (Psalm 78:24–25 NIV).

Fasting

They were able to eat heaven's grain, but their flesh wanted something different. In the next chapter, I am going to address this in more detail. But what they wanted to feed on wasn't what God wanted to give them. What they wanted was to be transported to Egypt through their smell and taste. Their hearts were still in Egypt. The flesh's desire is called concupiscence. This is a very strong desire, and the only way to shut it off is by feeding your spirit, rather than your flesh. You have to starve the Egyptian and his appetite within you! God told Moses that he wanted his people to meet with him in the desert so that they could worship him. What God was doing was taking them to where there was no earthly provision and only his provision for them. He was making them starve. He was taking away the Egyptian food and giving them heavenly food.

You have no idea the amount of preachers and even regular congregants that do not fast. It is mind-blowing to know that there are preachers that can go a whole year without doing a single fast. No time alone with God, no prayer, and especially, no fasting! This is insane to think about. Time alone with God through prayer and fasting is one of the ways to increase in the anointing of God. What fasting does is turns off the flesh and feeds the spirit. Fasting increases your spiritual appetite. It makes you want more of what God has for you. We must turn off the flesh. Prolonged period of time with your flesh activated is what keeps an open door for sin to come crouching and knocking at your door.

When was the last time you fasted? I'm not talking about a half-day fast. I'm not talking a fruit fast or fasting from things. I mean a fast where you don't eat, and you seek the Lord's presence. This is so needed today. We need a generation of believers that have purposed in their hearts that they are going to do whatever it takes to get to heaven! Remember, sin has an objective, and your flesh has an appetite. Don't just sit there and allow sin's goal to overtake you. Don't allow your flesh to eat. This is the time for your breakthrough!

4

Gluttony, the Acceptable Sin

This chapter is not going to be an easy one to accept. I say this because it was not easy for me either. I know that we tend to think that lust and sexual sin is the number one sin that plagues the world and the church, but I will go out on a limb and say that would not be a fair assessment. The number one sin in my humble opinion is gluttony. Humans do not need sex to survive, but they do need to eat. This necessity is what Satan has used to destroy countless people. He is currently doing it now.

No dancing, no sex, but lots of food

As I was coming up in the church, I was so into all that had to do with God and church. I was so in love with it all. It was a whole new world to me. It was all so new. It was quickly drilled into my head that premarital sex, drugs, drinking, cursing, and many other things were things and lifestyles Christians did not engage in. I was fine with it because I truly wanted God. I would do whatever it took to get me closer to the Lord. Of course, I was still struggling with pornography, masturbation, and lust, but I was trying. I got to a point where I was able to hide my battle with lust, but there was one battle I could not hide, gluttony.

I always played sports and led a very active lifestyle as I always tried to keep my body in great shape. As a child, I dealt with a very mild form of asthma, so being in shape and working out helped a lot. Now what I'm going to say is not putting the blame on anyone, but it certainly had a direct effect on my health. As I was in the church and learning from those that were in charge, I quickly stopped doing all the activities that I was used to. I was told that a lot of what I did was worldly. Looking back now, I can argue with what they considered worldly. I understand their intentions. They wanted me to be holy. I thank them for it because I wouldn't be the man that I am today if it wasn't for them. But this is where things go south for me.

Let's look at the culture that was before me. A vast majority of the ministers that I saw and knew were overweight and very out of shape. I didn't think much of it, but it started to be my reality as well. Dancing was sinful, so we couldn't dance. Drinking alcohol and doing drugs was sinful, so we couldn't drink. Premarital sex was sinful, so we couldn't do that. Going to the movie theaters was a sin because it meant to sit in the seat of scoffers. They would use this specific verse to justify not going: "*Blessed is the one who does not walk in step with the wicked or stand in the way that sinners take or sit in the company of mockers*" (*Psalm 1:1 NIV*).

So this meant we couldn't go to a movie theater, but we could go to restaurants where they openly served beer and liquor. I never understood this. Going to the beach was out of the question because there were people half-naked, and we couldn't be around that. Like I said, I didn't understand the why of some of these rules, but I didn't argue them because I would have done whatever it took to be right with God.

Now having said all that, there was one thing they never had an issue with or even talked about, and that was gluttony. We would have church functions and outings that would align with all of the rules of the church, and at every outing, we did what we were told, but at every function and outing, there was food. Lots and lots of food. Being of Puerto Rican heritage, there was amazing tasting food but not the healthiest.

We would eat and eat. The preachers would sit at their tables, condemn sin, and talk about the glory of God but fail to see that they, too, were sinning. I am not judging anyone, nor am I trying to shame anyone, but this is a truth and reality that no one wants to talk about. They would overindulge with food. They would eat two to three plates while they gained more weight. Their bellies would be so large they would be so winded when they preached that, at times, you would think that some of them would pass out while preaching. Many preachers suffered then and now from diabetes, hypertension, high blood pressure, heart attacks, and coronary heart disease, among many other weight-related illnesses. A study done by Lifeway Research finds that "forty-one percent of pastors are obese as compared to twenty-nine percent of all Americans." These numbers are not good at all, given what the Word of God stipulates for how we are to live our lives. But again, there was no dancing and no sex, but there were lots of food.

A slow death

This is an epidemic within the church, and no one is talking about it. The ministerial body of Jesus Christ is sick, well, not all, but many. Unfortunately, this issue is killing off many pastors and preachers very slowly and prematurely. The fact that the church is not talking about it as it should is contributing for the behavior to continue. This is what was starting to happen to me. I was gaining weight, and I could not stop it. In addition to growing in knowledge in the Word, I was also growing in physical size.

The God replacement

I was becoming what I was seeing. I not only developed an addiction to porn and lust, but I developed a seriously unhealthy addiction and relationship with food. This all started when I was a child. I can't really pinpoint a moment when it happened, but I do know why it started. I grew up seeing so many horrible situations in my family that it was easy for me to get lost in many worlds I built for myself as an escape. I began to lean on food as a comfort as do many people. I know how easy it can be.

Because I was so actively into sports and working out, I didn't notice it or even see it as a problem. My lifestyle allowed me to burn off the excess calories due to a high metabolism. But as everyone knows, age is the enemy for many. As we get older, our metabolisms slow down, making it harder for us to lose weight, especially if you're living a sedentary lifestyle. Whenever I would go through something, it would cause me to stress, and so I would refuge myself in food. It was my comfort. It was one of my escapes. So this behavior carried well into my ministerial career. I began to refuge myself in food, rather than God. Food was becoming my God, my idol, and peace.

I remember one time I was eating with people at the dinner table. As we were eating, I was not speaking to anyone. I remember catching myself smiling and so lost in my plate. When I looked up, everyone was staring at me. The look on their faces was of bewilderment. They couldn't believe how I was behaving with my food. I ate so fast. I ate as if I was obsessed. I was so embarrassed for myself, but I couldn't help it.

Fit or fat

By this time, the weight gain was noticeable. I could not hide the fat. I was getting to a point where it was uncomfortable. I was no longer going out with the rest of the youth and men to play basketball. I was no longer doing the activities that I once did to stay healthy because I wanted to "seek the Lord." That was my excuse. But in reality, I was out of shape and had no self-control. I couldn't control myself around food.

Discipline

I didn't know it then, but my mind was the problem. I didn't view food the way I should have viewed it. I was looking at food as fun and as an escape, rather than fuel. I got to a point where I would get angry if I didn't eat when I wanted to. I was not disciplined. On a ministry trip to Canada, a group of us from the church went to a church in Ontario. We ministered late into the night. When we got back to the house we were staying at, I was super-excited, thinking we were going to eat as was customary after ministering. Much to my surprise, there was nothing. All they offered was a piece of bread. I was really upset.

My mood changed. Embarrassingly, my mood change lasted until we left Canada. I am ashamed to say that me not being able to eat affected my ability to minister the Word of God. That was unacceptable. I let food change me. I let food stop me from ministering the Word of God. I stopped what God wanted to do because I couldn't eat. If I was disciplined, I would have eaten at an appropriate time in the day so that I could properly do what I had to do for the Lord. This testimony might not seem so impactful, but when food has the power to change you, your mood, and your mission, you know that there's a dangerous problem.

What does the Bible say?

The Bible is clear on food. Food is to be for fuel. It is to be for sustaining oneself. Not to overindulge in or to make as an idol. This is the issue with many preachers. We learn so much about every kind of sin and behavior, but we never address the most easily accessible sin: gluttony. The Bible says that gluttony is a sin. In my humble opinion, it is the number one sin that humans commit, and the most accepted and tolerated sin in the church. We talk about adultery, but we don't talk about gluttony.

Paul talks about being controlled by the impulses of the flesh through the stomach. This is not what should happen to someone that has been transformed by the renewal of their mind. Paul says this, *"Their destiny is destruction, their god is their stomach, and their glory is in their shame. Their mind is set on earthly things" (Philippians 3:19 NIV).*

We go back to Israel on this one. But before we do, let's take a look at what Paul's reason why these types of people are guided by and submissive to their stomachs. At the end of verse 19 of chapter 3, we see Paul say that "their mind is set on earthly things." For this, let's look at Israel while in the wilderness with Moses. *Exodus 16:3 states, "The Israelites said to them, 'If only we had died by the Lord's hand in Egypt! There we sat around pots of meat and ate all the food we wanted, but you have brought us out into this desert to starve this entire assembly to death.'"*

The people were hungry. In their desperation for food, they began to reminisce on what they left behind in Egypt. They remembered the pots of meat and all the food they ate and wanted. In Bible symbolism, Egypt represents the world. It (Egypt), being the world's greatest nation at the time, represents worldliness. It represents the world we were once slaves to. What they desired to eat was not heavenly. At that moment, they were not appreciative for their freedom. They wanted to eat from the world's plate. They wanted to eat the nourishment of the dominating aspect of their tripart makeup, which was their flesh. Their flesh was what was alive.

Yes, they were biologically Hebrew, but their hearts and stomachs were Egyptian. They correctly identified the plan of the Lord. The Lord's plan was starting to work. He was going to starve the Egyptian in them to death. The desire they had to eat food from Egypt was purely based on the fact that their flesh was in control. Just as Paul says, *"Their god was their stomach."*

Can't even fast

Having eating habits this way and so out of order, you might ask yourself, "When do they fast?" This is a fair question because it comes naturally to the mind when seeing someone that preaches the Word of God but is so overweight. Fasting is an essential part of our spiritual lives. It is how we grow in the spirit and kill off the desires of the flesh. It is how we increase in the anointing. When someone is in this condition, it is very hard to say no to food. Let's look at what makes it hard for someone to fast while in these conditions. According to a report by the University of Texas's MD Anderson Cancer Center:

- Overeating causes the stomach to expand beyond its normal size to adjust to the large amount of food. The expanded stomach pushes against other organs, making you uncomfortable. This discomfort can take the form of feeling tired, sluggish, or drowsy. Your clothes also may feel tight too.

- Eating too much food requires your organs to work harder. They secrete extra hormones and enzymes to break the food down.
- To break down food, the stomach produces hydrochloric acid. If you overeat, this acid may back up into the esophagus, resulting in heartburn. Consuming too much food that is high in fat, like pizza and cheeseburgers, may make you more susceptible to heartburn.
- Your stomach may also produce gas, leaving you with an uncomfortable full feeling.
- Your metabolism may speed up as it tries to burn off those extra calories. You may experience a temporary feeling of being hot, sweaty, or even dizzy.

Overeating makes it difficult for you to go through extended periods of no food. Since your stomach is expanded, it will always make you feel like you have to eat. This is very difficult to deal with during a fast.

Sleep is precious

As time went on, I was experiencing all of these things in my life. I was slowly but surely gaining weight, and I could not stop it. I was quickly entering a silent state of depression and embarrassment. I was no longer the person I once was and knew. The Bible says that when we are in Christ, we are a new creation. But I was turning into someone new that I didn't like. As time went on, I started to experience things in my sleep. I started to wake up with these terrible headaches that would last long into the day. I would soon find out they were called CO2 headaches. These headaches were the result of what I would later find out is called sleep apnea.

Sleep apnea is a condition that stops you from breathing while sleeping. There are two types of sleep apnea. One is called central sleep apnea. Central sleep apnea occurs because your brain doesn't send proper signals to the muscles that control your breathing. This is something that occurs naturally, and the person experiencing it did nothing to cause this. According to the Redwood Sleep Center, the second form of sleep apnea is called obstructive sleep apnea. This occurs when the muscles in the back of your throat relax. These muscles support the soft palate, the triangular piece of tissue hanging from the soft palate (uvula), the tonsils, the sidewalls of the throat and the tongue.

When the muscles relax, your airway narrows or closes as you breathe in. You can't get enough air, which can lower the oxygen level in your blood. Your brain senses your inability to breathe and briefly rouses you from sleep so that you can reopen your airway. This awakening is usually so brief that you don't remember it. You might snort, choke, or gasp. This pattern can repeat itself five to thirty times or more each hour, all night, impairing your ability to reach the deep, restful phases of sleep. The most common reason for sleep apnea in people is excessive weight and obesity. Being overweight is not just a physical health issue, but more importantly, it is a spiritual issue.

Prioritize

Let's look at what's really going on here. When someone is overweight and unhealthy, it eventually will directly affect the spiritual state of a person. No one just gets to being overweight overnight. It took time for you to put on all that weight. The change you are looking for is not found in a gym. It's not found in a fad diet nor is it found in a nutritionist. Your change is found in your desire to change. You have to be tired of the lack in your life. You have to truly desire to live in a place of abundance in God.

Lack of discipline and understanding of responsibility got you here. Now it's time to change it all with rearranging your priorities. This sounds harder than what it is, but I recognize that, for many, it can be one of the hardest things you will ever do. As a preacher, Christian, and follower of Christ, the order in which life is lived is of the utmost importance. What you put first in your life matters. Not prioritizing correctly will have you bow down to the wrong things in life and stand against the one person that truly matters.

Retrain the brain

Change is so desirable but yet so hard to know how to achieve. I briefly referenced this verse earlier in the chapter, but now I want to dissect it. Because I, like many, have done the same thing that I am about to mention. I have prayed countless prayers, asking God to help me with my weight without wanting to take and accept full responsibility for what I became. I'm sure many of you have prayed this, "Lord, please help me lose weight" then turn right around and eat a big huge burger or a really large, cheesy, greasy slice of pizza.

You tell yourself, "In the morning, I'm going to get up and go for a walk and burn some calories." But then when morning comes, you stay in bed, hitting the snooze button for a little more time of sleep. Trust me, we have all been there. You cannot change without retraining your mind. You have to truly think differently. You have to do exactly what the Bible says. You have to be renewed.

"Do not conform to the pattern of this world, but be transformed by the renewing of your mind. Then you will be able to test and approve what God's will is—his good, pleasing and perfect will" (Romans 12:2 NIV).

When Paul says to not conform to the pattern of this world, he is speaking about the times we are living in. The word *world* in the Greek means eons. The word *eons* means times and ages. I learned to do something with words that has given me great results for dissecting words. Split the words up. Con-form. Con means together, and form is shape. Essentially, Paul is telling us to not take the shape of the age and time that we are living in. It is easy to become our surroundings. It is easy to succumb to conformity due to the pressures around us. As kids, we knew this as peer pressure. We did whatever everyone around us was doing for fear of being the oddball. The pride of life is to live a life that looks so much like heaven that we stick out like a sore thumb down here on earth.

Paul goes on to tell us to be transformed by the renewal of our minds. Let's use the split method once more here. The word *transformed* comes from the Greek word *metamorphoō*, which is where we get the word metamorphosis. Trans-formed. Trans means to move, and formed means the finished shape of something. Paul masterfully tells us to move from form to form until we reach the finished and desired shape that God has eternally chosen for us through Christ. To do this is to change one's mind.

Sounds hard to do, huh? Changing the mind is the same as someone getting a software update on their phone or computer. Same hardware, but since it has new software, it will now behave differently. We do this by reading the Word. Reading the Word of God is literally downloading the mind of Christ in us. When you think something, you act it out. When you think something, you speak it. When you speak it, you do it. Reading of the Word daily will change our way of thinking, thus changing our words and actions. He finishes the verse with saying, "Then you will be able to test and approve what God's will is—his good, pleasing, and perfect will." This is so powerful and full of freedom because only when you are transformed and see things for what they are, are you able to see what God has chosen for your life. His perfect will that has no flaws in it. It is easy to lose ourselves in this battle. But God has given us the power to be called the sons of God. The sons of God eat from the table of heaven.

Convert the stomach

I had to literally stop eating! Now I am not advocating for one to starve themselves, but I am saying that your stomach cannot control you. I got to a point in my life where my obesity was truly affecting every aspect of my life. I could not preach without feeling like I was going to pass out. I got so tired of having my CPAP machine that I told myself I had enough. I was going to take back my life. I realized that if I could lose weight, I could do anything. I began to lose the weight and started to feel better. Being obese, I was not able to pray at the times in the morning that I was used to. It was cutting into my time with the Lord. I could not fast, pray, and neither could I read the Word without nodding off. My spiritual life was out of control, and I needed to regain control. I realized that God was not going to do it for me. I had to do it for myself with his grace.

This is a major factor in why many preachers sin. Many preachers and church members alike are overweight, especially here in the United States. This may sound comical, and I promise you that is not my intention here. But we are overweight. I used to ask myself how such an obese person could get all the women they got. Trust me, I asked myself the same question about myself. But looking back, I see why. I was soon in a world lost without God in the church. I said the right things, but my body and spirit said another. I had to convert my stomach from being Egyptian to Christian. Viewing food in the right manner will give you a clear level head about the Word of God. You can concentrate on God and his Word without that Egyptian appetite getting in the way.

5

Flying Under the Radar

The great God of the universe! The great I Am. The Creator of all that exists. Surely he can see all that happens on earth. I often wondered why God never exposed me during this period of my life. I wasn't fornicating with anyone, but I was bound to lust. It was always a mystery to me how God knew my condition but never publicly condemned me. I remember my pastor would announce that a special guest preacher was coming to the church to preach a sermon. I would be so fearful. I was so afraid of what God would do. I knew I was in sin. I knew I deserved to be exposed. You see, like clockwork, there was preaching of fear from the pulpit. They would preach the fear of God in us.

I would literally feel anxiety before going to the church service. Many times, I would pray and beg God not to expose me. I knew that God saw and knew everything that I was doing. I was so afraid to reveal who I really was. The addiction to porn grew stronger, and at this point in my life, I was so lost in it that I struggled inwardly with the presence of God. When he would move in my life, I felt so undeserving. That's how we should feel at all times. But this was different. I felt condemnation every time God would touch me. Every time he would do something in my life, I would feel like the worst person in the world. I couldn't enjoy his grace.

Fear tactics

For so long, this has been the strategy of many ministers. I was once such a hard preacher. I preached without mercy. It was a miracle that I would get invited back to certain places after having gone to a church and beat them up. I would not have mercy. I would preach about the problem and never offered the solution. I used to wonder why people wouldn't come up for prayer after I finished preaching. There were many awkward silences during and after I would deliver the message. Don't get me wrong, I would always preach the truth. A lot of the reactions I would get was due to the people doing exactly what I was preaching about.

But I preached without compassion, mercy, and love. I learned many years ago that truth is as deadly as a gun. The truth is to be administered as medicine, by a licensed professional, someone who knows how to handle the truth and deal it out for it to have the desired outcome. The apostle John speaks of how Jesus came. Jesus didn't just come down in his glory, telling everyone how it was. He never painted a picture with such a broad brush. He knew who to speak harshly to and who to speak lovingly to. He properly knew how to measure the time and place for the type of message he was to deliver. Let's take a look at what John said about Jesus.

"The Word became flesh and made his dwelling among us. We have seen his glory, the glory of the one and only Son, who came from the Father, full of grace and truth" (John *1:14 NIV*).

Jesus didn't just come and speak the truth. Jesus was full of truth. Not only was he full of truth, he was the truth. He spoke the full truth from the Father, but he also was full of grace. This is the part that many of us get wrong. Or should I say we lack? Jesus spoke the truth but also was full of grace. He knew his assignment and role. He knew who he was to come and rescue. He knew what their condition was. We are to preach the word of truth to convict the listener. Once they are convicted, we are to bring them to repentance through grace. Paul says in Ephesians 2:8, "For it is by grace you have been saved, through faith—and this is not from yourselves, it is the gift of

God." Paul says that by God's grace. This is the realization that we all must have. Grace is what saves us, not fear.

Adam, where are you?

But I know full well that conviction oftentimes causes fear in the heart of the offender. I am not blaming hard preaching as the reason why many do not confess their sins. But there has to be a clear healthy balance in the delivery of the message of the Lord. Let's go to the garden of Eden to take a closer look at this issue. God made Adam and Eve. He placed them in his garden. He placed them in a place of perfection. They were innocent of sin. They only knew the Lord. God gave them specific instructions on what they could eat. He told Adam that they were to not eat from the tree of good and evil.

"And the Lord God commanded the man, 'You are free to eat from any tree in the garden; but you must not eat from the tree of the knowledge of good and evil, for when you eat from it you will certainly die'" (*Genesis 2:16–17 NIV*).

God gave Adam the instructions before Eve was taken out of Adam. So although Eve was not present physically, she was in Adam and had to obey the same word. Eve sinning was the result of her not being with Adam. She gave to Adam to eat. When Adam eats, the completion of the sin was made because it was Adam who received the instructions and command. He knew what he did was wrong. He had the responsibility to correct Eve. As a result of this, Adam hid when he heard God come into the garden, looking for him.

It was the knowledge he had of the commands and also knowing who God was that made him hide. This wasn't the first meeting between God and Adam. Adam spent time with God enough to know his character, likes and dislikes. He hid. God came into the garden and asked, "Adam, where are you?" The spirit of fear was operating in the garden. This fear was keeping Adam from his freedom. God desired to have communion with Adam, but the fear kept Adam away from God. This is what the enemy of the souls is doing to many servants of God, keeping them in the darkness of their sin, making them believe that they cannot confess.

I lived like this for many years. Before I fell into adultery, I was living in darkness, afraid to confess who I was and what was living on the inside. The enemy managed to convince me that silence was the best way to go. I happily obliged.

Afraid to confess

Lately, we have been hearing the term "church hurt" more often. Now I am not trying to justify not confessing sin, but there are many reasons why this happens. The church atmosphere is directly related to this. When preachers stand on the pulpit, saying how God is going to reveal and unmask people for who they are, it leaves little room for someone to step forward and speak for themselves. Many times, I would sit in the service so scared because God was going to reveal my sin and issue. Now don't get me wrong, God did that and does that. It's still important for him to do that. But God is not an abuser.

God knows when to expose someone publicly. God's desire is for you to willingly confess your sins. I understand full well that not everyone does this, which is why he exposes people. But we the church have to create an atmosphere of confession. There has to be trust enough in the people and their leaders where they don't feel judged for speaking. It is the desire of every pastor for their members to willingly say what they did and, most importantly, what they are feeling.

It is our responsibility as pastors to create that atmosphere for them. I would hear people in the church say how God is going to do this and that. How he was going to hurt people on the altar for being in sin while their hearts and deeds privately were just as sinful or even worse. Not confessing my spiritual condition was a result of many things, one of which was the judgmental climate in the church. I thank God for my pastor. He was and is such a man of God. He dealt with me with such grace and mercy that it was the one reason that kept me in the church.

You see, I grew faithful to and revered more the wooden altar in the temple than the one in my heart. That is the one that God was after. He wasn't after the altar that we stood on to fake it. Some call it a stage, platform, or pulpit. Whatever you want to call it, it was not God's ultimate desire. He is after a heart. God doesn't live on a wooden platform. He desires to live inside hearts.

"Do you not know that your bodies are temples of the Holy Spirit, who is in you, whom you have received from God? You are not your own" (*1 Corinthians 6:19 NIV*).

If our bodies are temples, then we can safely say that the heart is his throne. God wants, through the Holy Spirit, to sit in our hearts and make his home in us. For us to achieve this, we have to do some cleaning. There has to be confession from the heart. God inspires Paul to write this in the fifth and eighth verses of the third chapter of Colossians.

"Put to death, therefore, whatever belongs to your earthly nature: sexual immorality, impurity, lust, evil desires and greed, which is idolatry" (Colossians *3:5 NIV*).

"But now you must also rid yourselves of all such things as these: anger, rage, malice, slander, and filthy language from your lips" (*Colossians 3:8 NIV*).

There are two phrases in these two verses that command us to do something. Put to death, and you must rid yourselves. These are commands that God is giving us to do. God will not do it for us. He has given us the power and grace to do so. How do you do this? By confessing it out of you.

For so long, I was so afraid to confess for fear of what people would say. I learned early on how unforgiving "church people" were. I remember hearing one of the church officials say from the pulpit that she didn't have mercy. That scared the confession right out of me.

An unforgiving church

What we read in the Bible is not what we see in many of our congregations. The Bible tells us how to deal with someone who is found to be in sin.

"Brothers and sisters, if someone is caught in a sin, you who live by the Spirit should restore that person gently. But watch yourselves, or you also may be tempted" (Galatians *6:1 NIV*).

This is the least that I saw. I saw a church that did not forgive the fallen; and when I say church, I'm speaking in general. The church of Jesus Christ was not a forgiving body as it should've been. I saw how they would gossip about someone who fell in the very sins they themselves were guilty of instead of praying for that person.

They placed stigmas and labeled someone for a sin committed and never looked at that person the same. I saw how they would treat someone based on past sins, forgetting their own sins. They would change the names of people and call them by their sin. The devil knows your name and calls you by your sin. God knows your sin and calls you by your name. This is so sad and disheartening. The church of Jesus Christ is the only army that attacks itself.

The spirit of fear

I spoke briefly about the spirit of fear in chapter two, but I want to shed some more light on this spirit. I want to show you what it does and how it operates. This type of spirit has the power to affect your imagination. The spirit of fear works by presenting you a false reality. It creates imaginations. Paul talks about this in 2 Corinthians 10:5, *"We demolish arguments and every pretension that sets itself up against the knowledge of God."* Paul uses the word *arguments*. The King James Version says imaginations. The word *imaginations* comes from the Greek word *logismos*. It means to reason. In this context, it is to reason as a way to the argument. In other words, it is debating with the knowledge you already know. What this spirit does is show you a false reality to argue against the truth that you already know of Christ. He is trying to make you believe something that does not exist.

This spirit was operating in my life and mind to keep me from confessing what was in my heart. One of the things he would show me was how I was going to be "sat down." The term sat down is a term used to describe disciplinary action taken on someone for sinful behavior or going against church rules and policy. The reason they used the term sat down is because you literally would sit down. You wouldn't be allowed to minister in the church in any capacity.

You wouldn't be allowed to participate from the altar, you wouldn't be allowed to serve, you wouldn't be allowed to even hold a tambourine in the church. It was shameful. Although some people today would say that is not right, but it is good to make someone take time out after failing morally in sinful behavior to reflect and get their heart right. I was so afraid of this.

The spirit of shame

I also spoke briefly about this spirit in chapter 2 as well, but I also would like to dig a little deeper on it. This spirit of shame specializes in keeping you away from the presence of God. It also keeps you from doing the will of God while you're in the church. In the garden of Eden, one of the things that Adam says to God is telling of this. He tells God that he knew he was naked and hid himself.

"He answered, 'I heard you in the garden, and I was afraid because I was naked; so I hid" (*Genesis 3:10 NIV*).

Oftentimes, in the Bible, God uses nakedness to describe shame. He uses it in dreams, as well to convey a shameful feeling upon someone.

When Adam saw that he was naked, he chose to hide. His choosing to leave the place that he and God would customarily meet was a sign that he felt shame. That is the operation of shame. Shame is a spirit that not only condemns you but also makes you go back into the law and abandon grace. The meeting place with God was a place of grace. Because if nakedness meant sin and shame, then him meeting God in that state was God pouring grace over Adam, despite his situation. Shame makes you feel unworthy of God's forgiveness.

I was so afraid to let the real me out, so I did not confess. At this point, I am a few years into seeking the Lord and attending church regularly. I was a part of the church family. God was showing up in my life, and things were happening. I was starting to climb up in the church. I got to a point in my life where I felt like absolutely no one could see my condition. I felt as if I was flying under the radar. There were times that I knew God was letting me know that he was watching. But as far as I knew, no one knew anything or could suspect anything.

This is far too common in the church. There is such good talk of the gifts and that God reveals. But in reality, the better question is this, why do we want God to reveal? Do we want God to reveal so that the person can be set free from sin, and they can be saved? Or do we want God to reveal their sin so that they can be destroyed to validate us as prophets?

Prophets like Jonah

In the Word of God, a prophet named Jonah was just like this. He was upset with God for God telling him to go to Nineveh, to preach and prophesy that there was judgment coming from God to them. He was so upset that he chose to run away from his assignment. He went so far as to get in a ship and hide in the downstairs part of the ship. The ship encountered some rough seas due to a storm that was caused by his disobedience. His gripe with God was that he knew that once he relayed God's message to Nineveh, he would forgive them. Seems as though he had experienced God's mercy and grace toward people he prophesied to before. His inability to embrace God's forgiveness for people showed a lack of love and a lack of empathy for the people he preached to. Preacher, consider that the people you are preaching to are also loved by God.

Undetected but suspected

Living like this for so long was exhausting. Believing I wasn't able to confess to the mess that lived inside my heart was exhausting. It was exhausting trying to keep up with an image God never intended for me. You see, in order for me to go undetected, I had to do what was expected of me. I had to live religiously, instead of relationally. I was in religion but not in relationship. In my mind, I was undetected, but in reality, I was definitely suspected.

I was suspected by the few true men and women of God in the church and churches I would go to minister to. Let me explain. There was always this weird strange look in the faces of some people after hearing me preach. Even before I would preach, there were people that could see right through me. I could feel it. I knew they knew what was in me. My spirit could feel how they knew what was underneath the splendor of anointing and ministry. I was able to fool many but not the few that really prayed.

It's the same to God

At this point, I wasn't in adultery yet, but I was addicted to porn and lust. So it was the same. Many of us Christians deceive ourselves by thinking that as long as we don't do it, we are good. But as you know, grace is harder than the law. In the law, you had to have done the deed to be found in sin. But in grace, the act is just a manifestation of what lies beneath. Jesus mentions in one of his preachings that even a lustful look is equal to laying down with the woman.

"But I tell you that anyone who looks at a woman lustfully has already committed adultery with her in his heart" (Matthew 5:28 NIV).

This is the reality for many preachers and Christians. I know it sounds like I am bashing and tearing down the ministerial body, and I promise you that is not my intention. I am just shedding light on what is truly happening behind closed doors that most people and churches so nonchalantly just sweep under the rug. This is a travesty, and it truly has to stop. We have to bring transparency back to the altar of the Lord.

The anointing covers the mess

As I was getting known in the church circuit, I would hear news of fellow colleagues in the ministry being found in moral failure, be it adultery, fornication, lying, stealing, domestic violence, etc. It was always a shocker to everyone who heard it. Why, you might ask? Because the most anointed people are the messiest in the Gospel of Jesus Christ. Now let me explain before I get attacked here.

The mess of a preacher usually is not intentional. It is the fleshly human struggle they are so desperately trying to overcome. But what happens most of the time is that the church or the crowd tends to elevate a preacher because of the spiritual gifts they manifest. We forget that the gift does not mean being right with God. Jesus said:

> And these signs will accompany those who believe: In my name they will drive out demons; they will speak in new tongues; they will pick up snakes with their hands; and when they drink deadly poison, it will not hurt them at all; they will place their hands on sick people, and they will get well. (Mark 16:17–18 NIV)

Instead, the church is after the signs. The church is after the prophet of the moment. Whatever man or woman comes along displaying gifts, signs, and wonders, we flock to as if we have never seen these things before. This means that the supernatural isn't so natural in many people's lives. This shouldn't be. We should be accustomed to seeing God show up in our lives on a daily basis.

So what this causes is for so many preachers and Christians to go undetected because of the anointing. The anointing is the focus and center of attention, rather than the condition of the person. The condition of the person certainly matters. I'm sure that many will debate this and say that the Word of God will not turn back void, and I agree. But the integrity of the Gospel has such an impact in the world. The sins and falls of a preacher affect the Gospel as a whole.

I remember when a pastor friend of mine was caught in a rather embarrassing and compromising scandal. I was asked about it from someone. We spoke about the matter briefly, and she told me this statement that resonated with me. She said, "Too much content and not enough character." This was so impactful to me because we tend to overlook the heart and condition because the preacher can call out names and phone numbers without knowing anyone in the room.

God always reveals

So here I was, preaching now, a young man eager and hungry to travel and preach the Word of God, desiring to tell the world about a God who can set them free while still bound himself. After all of this, what I didn't realize is that God was revealing himself to me and my condition all along. I thought I was getting away with it. But in reality, God was being patient with me. Looking back now, I can remember those times when God would speak to me about my condition, and I would choose to ignore it.

I would literally only focus on the powerful prophecies concerning my calling, not understanding that calling came with a price. You have to understand that nothing stays hidden from the Lord, nothing stays in darkness. All things will eventually come out. God will deal with everything in that day of judgment.

"For there is nothing hidden that will not be disclosed, and nothing concealed that will not be known or brought out into the open" (Luke 8:17 NIV).

"For God will bring every deed into judgment, including every hidden thing, whether it is good or evil" (Ecclesiastes 12:14 NIV).

<h1 style="text-align:center">6</h1>

Public Victories and Private Defeat

By this time, I am now in my early twenties, and I am very good at preaching. God is using me, and I was achieving all of the ministerial goals I set out for myself. I was getting known around the different states on the East Coast. I graduated from a biblical institute. I was starting to be many churches' choice as a preacher for many events and services.

Now before I was a preacher, I was a musician and also a singer. I was the worship leader in the church. Through the music ministry, I was able to get known. I would get invited to sing and play music. They would later see that I also preached. That's how it began. Early on, the Lord spoke to me and told me that he was going to bless me in the music. I was going to travel the world, and that I would be known as an artist for him. I, like many do, created a plan for my life based on what he told me. I planned out every step and stage in my life. I developed my own five-year plan.

Satanic interference

Whenever the Lord makes a proclamation over someone's life as powerful as it is, it's piercing through from the spiritual world to the natural world. Before something happens in the physical realm, it has to first happen in the spiritual realm. Nothing earthly precedes the spiritual. God declares his decrees and edicts in the spiritual, and then in time, it is manifested in the natural. I'll give an example of what I mean.

In Daniel, chapter 10, the angel was sent before him to manifest in the natural what was already set in the spiritual.

"Then he continued, 'Do not be afraid, Daniel. Since the first day that you set your mind to gain understanding and to humble yourself before your God, your words were heard, and I have come in response to them'" (Daniel 10:12 NIV).

In this same way, Satan and his demonic kingdom is able to hear the prophecies spoken over God's people. The prince of Persia fought the angel that was sent to give Daniel the word that he needed to hear from God. This is exactly what happens today. Satan and his demonic spirits are listening. Once they get wind of what God is doing, they make their attempt to interfere with the Lord's plans.

They set up booby traps! I know, you haven't heard that term in a long time, probably since you were a child. But that is exactly what he does. He sets up traps for you to fall in to interfere with God's plan. He will place things in your life to confuse you, to trick you and fool you, to make you believe that what he has placed in your life is what God is giving you. Unfortunately, many have been deceived by this satanic tactic. He takes advantage of the fact that many in the church do not pray. Prayer is connection and vision. When you're praying, you're able to see and hear what the throne of God has planned for you.

We usually see this tactic play out in the lives of single Christians. They are so intent on being with someone. Oftentimes at the time when someone shows up in their lives, they are weak from waiting that they accept anyone that comes along. The enemy shows up when you're tired and hungry. That's when many let their guard down. Overlooking the red flags in a person is a common issue when looking for a partner. Because Satan knows this, he will plant what God has spoken over your life.

Satan interfered in my life. He planted people in my life to try and deter me from what God predestined for me. Just as I described, I stopped praying. I was not connected, and I had no vision for what

God was saying and doing in my life. I was doing what many do and did. They were led by the gift and not the voice of God.

Talent is not enough

I do not mean to be braggadocios about myself, but for the sake of telling my story, I have to be straightforward about who I am. I can recognize what God has given me to work for him and his kingdom. God has blessed me with many talents and abilities. He has given me a mind for music and creativity. Over the years, I became a professional musician, music producer, singer, songwriter, composer, arranger, and professional photographer/videographer. He gave me so much in the world of creativity.

Now because of this, I became very valuable to many people and churches. Since I wasn't praying the way I needed to, I let myself be led by my talent, rather than the Spirit of God. This reminds me of a story in the Bible that speaks of this very issue. I could've gotten out of this with just confessing my condition, but because I felt I was in too deep, I somehow convinced myself in keeping quiet. I had no idea how bad of an idea that was.

> And he went with them. They went to the Jordan and began to cut down trees. As one of them was cutting down a tree, the iron ax-head fell into the water. "Oh no, my Lord!" he cried out. "It was borrowed!" The man of God asked, "Where did it fall?" When he showed him the place, Elisha cut a stick and threw it there, and made the iron float. (2 Kings 6:4–6 NIV)

There is so much here to dissect. You see, as Elisha and the prophets were building a place for them to stay and a school for the prophets, one of the workers, as he was cutting down a tree with an ax, yelled. He yelled because as he was cutting, the ax-head fell in the water. This is so important because wood can't cut down wood. When the ax-head fell in the water, he was left with a piece of wood in his hands. Although the wooden handle was important, it was not what cut down the tree. The most important part of the tool was no longer there.

That's how it was for me and many preachers. I was not operating with the most important part of what I did, the Spirit of God. I was moving about with just talent. I was trying to cut down trees with just wood. Just as wood can't cut down wood, demons don't cast out demons. Flesh can't operate godly spiritual issues. Talent is not enough. My ability to do many things well that others couldn't do allowed me to appear so powerful and victorious, but little did they know that I was living a private life of defeat.

Things were getting out of control

My addiction to porn was at an all-time high. It was out of control, and porn was starting to not be enough for my lustful hunger. I was now at the point where I would watch porn in the morning, afternoon, and night. I would watch it before I even went to church. I wouldn't go a day without it while publicly touting a life of victory. I was the biggest fraud. Masturbation was an everyday occurrence. The way I viewed women was horrible, and my prayer life was virtually nonexistent.

I wish I could say that this is not a common occurrence in the church, but this is far more common that we would like to admit. The amount of pastors, clergymen, and church members addicted to pornography is staggering, men and women alike. The following is an excerpt from a report done primarily by the Barna Group and Covenant Eyes, and it reveals:

1. Over forty million Americans are regular visitors to porn sites. The average visit lasts six minutes and twenty-nine seconds.
2. There are around forty-two million porn websites, which totals around 370 million pages of porn.

3. The porn industry's annual revenue is more than the NFL, NBA, and MLB combined. It is also more than the combined revenues of ABC, CBS, and NBC.
4. Forty-seven percent of families in the United States reported that pornography is a problem in their home.
5. Pornography use increases the marital infidelity rate by more than 300 percent.
6. Eleven is the average age that a child is first exposed to porn, and 94 percent of children will see porn by the age of fourteen.
7. Fifty-six percent of American divorces involve one party having an "obsessive interest" in pornographic websites.
8. Seventy percent of Christian youth pastors report that they had at least one teen come to them for help in dealing with pornography in the past twelve months.
9. Sixty-eight percent of churchgoing men and over 50 percent of pastors view porn on a regular basis. Of young Christian adults, eighteen to twenty-four years old, 76 percent actively search for porn.
10. Fifty-nine percent of pastors said that married men seek their help for porn use.
11. Thirty-three percent of women, aged twenty-five and under, search for porn at least once per month.
12. Only thirteen percent of self-identified Christian women say they never watch porn—87 percent of Christian women have watched porn.
13. Fifty-five percent of married men and 25 percent of married women say they watch porn at least once a month.
14. Fifty-seven percent of pastors say porn addiction is the most damaging issue in their congregation. Sixty-nine percent say porn has adversely impacted the church.

Performers

The truly scary part of this is that many preachers manage to learn to minister in this condition. Many ministers learn how to become performers, rather than ministers. I did exactly this. Now I don't want you to read this and think that I didn't care about my spiritual condition. It truly was front and center in my life and mind. I can say that I loved the Lord. Yes, I loved the Lord. I was just afraid of his people. I was afraid to face the music.

So in order to escape what I feared, I had to learn to perform to satisfy the religious requirements expected of a minister. I quickly learned the right words to make everyone believe that I was on the level. I learned the behaviors. I learned to do what many people do in many congregations, which is sweep things under the rug. As long as it wasn't public, it didn't have to be dealt with. So I put on a show. I performed so well I was accepted among the elite. I was taken in because I sounded just like them.

Commonality

The Word of God says in Romans 5:12, *"Therefore, just as sin entered the world through one man."* We all have commonality with one another, whether we are believers and nonbelievers—sin. We all have inherited sin because of the disobedience of Adam. It would be foolish to believe that someone who is tremendously and wonderfully used by God would not have fleshly struggles. We all share in the sin of Adam. It is important for all believers, even those that are not in the fivefold ministry, to understand that no one has it down right. The only thing we can have down is our search for Christ and his Holy Spirit.

I would see how certain people in the church would truly struggle with their flesh. They would always fall into destructive behavior, especially those who God would make a public calling on. I remember coming up in the youth group, there was one youth that had so much potential. He was one of the musicians of the church. He was the leader of the youth. He would always struggle in the flesh. On the outside looking in, he was good. But because I was going through the same thing, I knew what he was going through. The only difference between him and I was that I was able to hide my condition better.

A godly exposure is necessary

I mentioned earlier in this chapter that I was worried and afraid that God would expose me. But him exposing me is exactly what I needed. You have to understand that darkness is what sin and the devil need to remain in a life. As long as something is hidden in darkness, it goes undetected. This is why the enemy loves to operate in darkness. This is how the enemy is able to go undetected for so many years in the lives of so many.

> Everyone who does evil hates the light, and will not come into the light for fear that their deeds will be exposed. But whoever lives by the truth comes into the light, so that it may be seen plainly that what they have done has been done in the sight of God. (John 3:20–21 NIV)

A united kingdom

This is a tactic Satan and his dark kingdom have used for thousands of years. They work together. You never see the kingdom of darkness divided. They work together to keep you bound. Demonic spirits work in conjunction with one another to carry out the orders of the enemy of the souls to keep God's creation down and bound. This is why so many Christians struggle to get loose of the grasp of the devil. They fail to realize that they have to destroy the problem and defeat the enemy at the root.

Jesus speaks of this in the gospels. In *Matthew 12:25–26, it says:*

> Jesus knew their thoughts and said to them, "Every kingdom divided against itself will be ruined, and every city or household divided against itself will not stand. If Satan drives out Satan, he is divided against himself. How then can his kingdom stand?"

This is crucial for you to live a life of victory, not only in public but also in private.

The root

You have to go to the root of the chain that the enemy is using to enslave you. Jesus went a little further with this in the previous passage.

"Or again, how can anyone enter a strong man's house and carry off his possessions unless he first ties up the strong man? Then he can plunder his house" (Matthew 12:29 NIV).

In this case, the strong man is what I am calling the root spirit or the principal spirit. This is the spirit that first came in to give way to the spirit I call the manifesting spirit or the symptom spirit. These are the spirits that are operating on the outside. The one's that are clearly visible. So in order to get rid of these spirits and issues in your life, you have to work from the beginning. Otherwise, you will be going in circles treating the manifesting symptom, instead of the root cause of the issue. Below is a diagram to better explain what I mean.

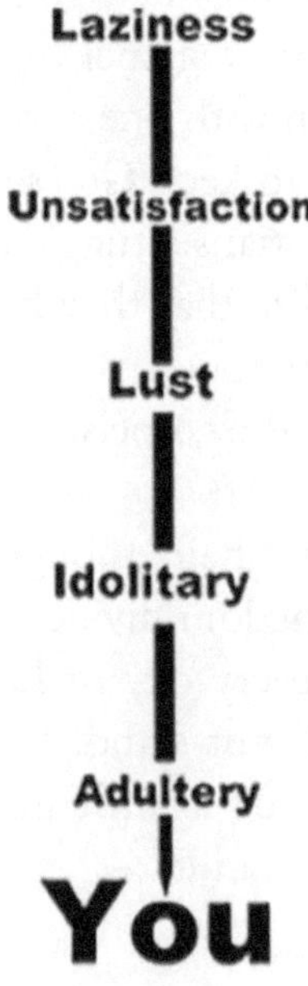

You have to know how to identify the issue properly. Living a life of private defeat is due to not dealing with the root issues in our lives. I lived this way for years. I was so good at going from victory to victory before the people. I went from victory to victory before my pastor and church. It was only so that I can keep appearances. But privately, after a preaching or a local church service, I would come home to the internal war and struggle that I found myself a slave to. I would preach and appear victorious on the pulpit, but then when I would go back to my hotel room or home, I would fall victim to the temptation to the spirit of masturbation and to watch porn.

Triumphant freedom

This is not what God called us for. This is not the life that God has predestined for us to live. He desires for us to live a life of freedom. Not just a life of freedom, but to live in our freedom triumphantly. Throughout the entire Bible, especially in the New Testament, God shows us that through the obedience and victory of Christ, we are able to overcome what was once impossible through the law. Paul says it like this, *"For what the law was powerless to do because it was weakened by the flesh, God did by sending his own Son in the likeness of sinful flesh to be a sin offering. And so he condemned sin in the flesh"* (Romans 8:3 NIV).

A frustrated prayer life

Living triumphantly does not mean that you no longer sin. It means that although you're still in this fleshly body, you are able to live the way God intended you to live. You are able to say what was once impossible for you to say... *No!* You are able to say the word no to the temptations that come to your life. To say no to the urges and impulses of the flesh was so hard and virtually impossible for me. I was a slave to whatever thought and feeling that came to mind.

I couldn't go a day without failing God. My prayers were so routine and redundant. I would pray the same prayer, day in and day out; well, that is whenever I got around to pray. My prayer life was a frustrated one. I would turn on TBN, Daystar, and other Christian stations, even radio stations, the way they presented serving God seemed so easy. I couldn't understand how people could just live so free as if they had no struggles in their lives. I didn't understand that prayer wasn't for me to just ask for God to do things for me.

Prayer for me was a way to be emptied of myself and connect to God. It was for me to be able to open my eyes and see in the spirit realm of God, to know what he wanted for me. I had to understand that prayer was for me to be able to cry out and for God to guide me to a place of calmness in him.

"When hard pressed, I cried to the Lord; he brought me into a spacious place" (*Psalm 118:5 NIV*).

It's okay to not be okay

In the church, being in victory was the thing to say. When someone would ask you how you were doing or how you were feeling, you were expected to say, in a convincing tone, "In victory." Despite you feeling down, despite you feeling defeated, despite you arriving to church after watching porn, you were expected to say that you were in victory or else you would be shamed in a winded lecture that, instead of lifting you up, made you feel like you were a failure.

This was what I went through. I had to always say I was in victory. I couldn't say that I was struggling. Now I'm not blaming people. By no means is that my intention. What I am saying is that this was the atmosphere and culture. There was no room for being human and weak. It took me years to understand that I didn't have to have it all down. It took me years to understand that it was okay for me to come to church where I'm barely hanging on. The house of God is where we are to go and leave it all. The Word of God says for us to present our bodies as living sacrifices. We are to take all of what and who we are to God. I often say to my congregation that church is the right place for the wrong people. Take all of yourself to the Lord. It's okay to struggle. You have to keep in mind that you're human and will mess up. Just make sure when you mess up you take your mess up to the Lord.

7

Marriage Won't Fix It

I, like many people, desired what God has designed for all of us. I wanted to be married, have children, and a home. I wanted what I thought was impossible for me because I never saw a clear example at home of what a healthy family looked like. I grew up in a very broken home. I did not grow up with my biological father. He and my mother split up before I could remember. So I never truly had a male figure in my life to show me how a man is supposed to be in the home.

So I never focused on marriage or even thought about being married. That was the TV life. I always said, as a joke, that the television raised me. As I mentioned in chapter 1, because of the circumstances in my home, I and my siblings had to be split up to live with different family members. Looking back, they did this to not have us go through foster care. I am grateful to God that they took us all in. My grandparents' form of instructing me was sitting me in front of the television for hours. So television raised me. I'm laughing as I am writing this.

The love of my life

I'm now in my early twenties, and I started to date who would later become my wife, while still dealing with my lust issue. I thought to myself that she was who I wanted to marry. But since I was in such a ministry atmosphere, I wanted what many ministers wanted.

I wanted a ministry partner, rather than a life partner. I wanted to marry someone that was a good fit for ministry, instead of being a good fit for my life. Ministry is great, but it's not everything. The biggest mistake a minister can do is look for ministerial qualities in someone, instead of life qualities.

We dated for three years. She was also a worship leader. She was and still is an amazing singer/worshipper. We were on the worship team at church together. We traveled, we preached, we ministered together for years, before we were ever a couple. We were a great ministry duo, but we both neglected to look at the life qualities. I hid my lust and porn addiction from her. I look back and feel like I tricked her into believing I was someone else. I wanted to be fixed. I wanted my issue to go away.

Since prayer wasn't fixing it because I was praying wrong, I thought that marriage would somehow fix it. My thinking was, *If I have married sex, which would be okay with God, then I can satisfy the urges and impulses and not sin against God.* That was the biggest lie and deception I have ever told to myself. I know that I am not alone in this frame of thought.

Marrying for the wrong reasons

I have spoken to countless men and women about this, and the answers I got, most of the time were the same. Many people would say that they married too early. Others begrudgingly admitted to marrying for the wrong reasons, believing that their struggles with porn and lust would end when they got married. Sadly enough, it doesn't fix it. This is when many confuse love for lust. They marry out of lust, rather than love. Eventually, the lust wears off, and they're left with the person, not the body. You're left with their mind and soul. This is where people feel feelings of disillusion.

They begin to feel and see that the marriage they are in is not what they truly wanted. That is what lust does. This is a spirit. The spirit of lust has the power to make you forget and ignore. It will make you forget what God has spoken over your life, and it will make you ignore the nudging and voice of the Holy Spirit in your life. This is when, in many cases, the door to adultery is opened. In my case, not everything I mentioned is what happened to me. But I can say that I definitely did not marry for the right reasons. I did love my wife, but I was not healed.

Selfish union

There is also the case for those who marry for selfish reasons. When we marry for selfish reasons, we become takers, rather than givers. The best marriages are when two givers come together. In retrospect, I can say that I was a taker and not a giver. I took in every aspect. I took financially, spiritually, emotionally, and sexually. I took financially because I was a lazy man. I would get fired from every job I got.

I took spiritually because it was always all about me and what God was doing in and with me. I didn't take the time to pastor my wife. I took from her emotionally because I never validated her feelings. It was always about how I felt and how she made me feel. I took from her sexually because I looked to satisfy myself instead of making sure she was satisfied. I took and took until the devil came to take from me.

Two becoming one

Understand that a marriage essentially is two worlds merging and becoming one. Everything that your husband/wife is exposed for you to take in as your own. You are now having to become one with all that they are. You will not only take in the good but also the bad. Oh yes, there's bad. I would say that in a marriage, it seems that there are more bad moments than good. But the good moments always outweigh the bad moments. The Bible says this, *"That is why a man leaves his father and mother and is united to his wife, and they become one flesh"* (Genesis *2:24 NIV*).

Becoming one flesh is the goal of a marriage, just as Jesus said that he and the Father are one. Eve came from Adam. When God created Adam, he created Eve at the same time. You see, just like you and I were in God since before he laid the foundations of the world, Eve was in Adam. God created Adam but manifested Eve. A husband finding his wife is the manifestation of what was already in place. When a godly man and a godly woman marry, they are simply manifesting what God has stipulated since before the beginning of time.

"So they are no longer two, but one flesh. Therefore what God has joined together, let no one separate" (Matthew 19:6 NIV).

Here in this verse, it says, "*What God has joined together.*" That means that it's a godly thing. God puts the marriage together. What that also means is that before we marry, we ought to make sure that

- it is God putting the marriage together;
- we are with the right person;
- we are getting married for the right reasons;
- we have to make sure we are getting married at the right time.

Never enter into marriage being unsure. Your spouse will eventually feel your insecurity. It will only cause pain and resentment—emotions that are very difficult to overcome.

You are your spouse's keeper

When you marry someone, you are no longer alone. You are now half of a team. You are half of a singular life that comprises two people. You are not to think of just yourself anymore. You are to be the provider, protector, and defender of their cause. The man is supposed to provide love, and the woman is supposed to provide respect.

Discovery

It was in all this that I found out who I was. Marriage didn't take anything away. What it actually did was expose all that I was. Yes, I knew who I was, but I did not know all that was in my heart. God will use people, places, and things to expose what's in our hearts. We often get angry with the negative things that happen to us. But when you look at how the Lord actually operates, you begin to understand that, many times, it is through traumatic situations that many of the underlying issues come to the surfaces. The desire of the Lord is for us to walk in our victory and healing. Unfortunately, oftentimes the road to get to victory and healing goes through some really dark places.

Drifting apart

The desired goal of a marriage, especially a healthy one, is to grow together, to get closer to each other as the days, weeks, months, and years pass by. To do this, there has to be constant communication and a willingness to spend time together to hear the other person out. This shouldn't be difficult to do, but it tends to be. This was happening to my marriage. At first, we got together wanting to spend every second together. We lived for Saturday mornings where we would get up early and go to a diner or a restaurant to eat breakfast together, spend time in each other's presence. It was great. But as time went on, we started to focus on the bad things.

My wife was in school to get her bachelor's degree. I was working full-time while in my pursuit for success in ministry. Things seemed great, but, secretly, we were drifting apart. The breakdown began to happen with our prayer lives. How could we not drift apart if we were already drifting apart from God? The famous quote "A couple that prays together, stays together" is true. We didn't pray together. We didn't study the Word together. We did not look like what we presented in front of the congregation as worship leaders and preachers.

Eventually, the spiritual drought in our prayer lives caught up to our married lives. This is the danger of not having God in the center. God is who keeps a marriage together. When God is the center of a marriage, the entire existence of that marriage is to please the Lord. They grow in faith together. They seek to please one another in the presence of the Lord.

Satan is looking for a way in

During this period of our marital breakdown, we began to experience many fights. We started to argue and bicker like it was a requirement to stay with each other. It was getting to be a nonstop, everyday thing. We were told that the first five years of marriage were the toughest, and I believed it. We were not understanding what was happening. When you live a life out of the Spirit, with no prayer, you are blinded to what is truly happening around you in the spirit realm. You fail to see that things that happen in life aren't just random situations and circumstances. Many, and I mean many of the things that happen in this realm originate in the spirit world. Demonic spirits are out to destroy and stop the children of God.

"For our struggle is not against flesh and blood, but against the rulers, against the authorities, against the powers of this dark world and against the spiritual forces of evil in the heavenly realms" (Ephesians 6:12 NIV).

You might think that argument with your husband/wife is them coming against you or being rude, angry, and confrontational. But, remember, that it is not them. It is a demonic spirit trying to disrupt the peace in your marriage, home, and family. Always remember that we do not wrestle against people. People are not the enemy. Paul tells us in Ephesians 6:12 that our struggle is not against flesh and blood.

They are not your enemy

A quick way to end an argument or quarrel between you and your spouse is to understand that it is not them. Keep in mind that there is a demonic spirit looking to disrupt the peace that God has provided, the peace that surpasses all understanding. This is so freeing because you can put down your weapon. You can take down the image the enemy places on your spouse of being the enemy and embrace them as your ally. When people rise against you, remember that it's not them. It is a demonic spirit rising up against you. When you are married, you are each other's partner.

We have an enemy

You have to know that we have an enemy. He is not human. He is not of this world. He is intent on destroying everything that God has his hand on. I want to reiterate that your spouse is not the enemy. Your spouse is not out to destroy you. You might say I don't know your story. But if you pray, you will be able to see who is truly at work. The Bible says in *1 Peter 5:8 (NIV), "Be alert and of sober mind. Your enemy, the devil prowls around like a roaring lion looking for someone to devour."* The Bible clearly calls him our enemy. He is not for us. He is 100 percent against us. His entire reason for being is to oppose us. You will see how the enemy came in through an open door that you allowed for him to get in through.

Doors are open

Doors are opened when we do not take care of what God has given us to take care of. When we become negligent of our spiritual lives, the enemy of the souls is able to infiltrate covertly. Usually, when he is in, you wouldn't know it until it's too late. A door is access to a separate room or access into a place or building. It is important to do a self-check of our spiritual lives. We must assess what access the enemy of the souls has in our lives. What doors have you opened? What doors do you have unguarded? You do this by speaking to your spouse and confessing to them what is in your heart. Your marriage is potentially exposed, and access may be given to what is against it.

Windows

Imagine a building, designed for military purposes. The building has windows all over it, and they're all open. It is where the generals go to plan their next attack on their enemy. Suddenly, the enemy attacks that building. Ask yourself, how did the enemy know what they were doing? How could they see the plans that were being formulated? The enemy was able to see inside and know the plans. He was able to plan against the generals, all because the windows were open.

With all the windows open, the generals are exposed to all of the espionage the enemy is doing to later use it against them. This is why being able to see through windows and shutting your windows is so important. Windows are those behaviors that let people and demons know what is going on in the inside. Believe it or not, we give off signals to our enemy that let him know what condition our spiritual lives are in. He absolutely does not have the ability to see or read our thoughts, but he is good at reading our behavior.

Prayer

The ability to see is crucial for being able to defend against attacks. This is what prayer is. Prayer is connection. Prayer is vision. When you pray, you are crossing over from the natural realm to the supernatural realm. In prayer, you are able to see what is not seen in the natural. This is why a healthy prayer life is so important in a marriage. For a marriage to stay together, there needs to be prayer, not just praying as an individual, but praying together as a couple.

Praying together as a couple will keep you both vigilant and alert to the attacks of the enemy. You are each other's watchman. The Word of God shows how prayer can open the eyes of someone under siege.

> When the servant of the man of God got up and went out early the next morning, an army with horses and chariots had surrounded the city. "Oh no, my Lord! What shall we do?" the servant asked. "Don't be afraid," the prophet answered. "Those who are with us are more than those who are with them." And Elisha prayed, "Open his eyes, Lord, so that he may see." Then the Lord opened the servant's eyes, and he looked and saw the hills full of horses and chariots of fire all around Elisha. (2 Kings 6:15–17 NIV)

My wife was feeling it

During all this time, I was lost in my own lust and issues that I thought I had my wife fooled. I thought she didn't know what I was going through. I had the same mentality with her that I had at church. I felt I needed to hide my struggle because I thought she wouldn't understand me. The biggest lie I told myself was that she didn't know what was going on. I fooled myself into believing that because I "got away with it" at church, that I somehow was getting away with it at home, in my marriage. I was wrong.

My wife was absolutely feeling it. She knew something was wrong. She could sense that things weren't right. Many a times I would sneak off into the next room to go watch porn. I would be in the next room for hours, watching porn on the computer, as shameful and embarrassing as that sounds. I was so confused as to why I was still addicted to pornography when I was married. What I didn't understand is that the addiction does not break because of something. It breaks because of someone, and that someone's name is Jesus.

My wife was feeling my distance. She was feeling my silence. She was feeling the darkness living within my heart. I didn't know it, but she knew I was dealing with lust. She just didn't know how to tell me she knew. She grew up as a nonconfrontational person and, therefore, did not know how to address what she knew and what she was feeling. She just knew that her husband was broken. I spent many nights not sleeping next to my wife, all because lust had control over me, especially at night.

A preacher's nighttime lust

I would have these uncontrollable nighttime lust struggles. I would burn in my lust at night. It was such a fight. I struggled with my flesh, and more often than not, my flesh would win. There were many days where I was good during the day. But, at night, I would fall prey to my flesh. I gave in without a fight; and when I would fight it, I wouldn't stand a chance. I thought I was alone in this. But after talking to many people and ministers, I quickly saw that I was not alone. There were many, and I mean many preachers and ministers that went through this. Imagine if ministers go through this, imagine how many church members go through this.

At night, the body is dormant. The body is stationary, but the mind is still active. While the body is stationary, the mind is still able to receive information. This is when spirits have the ability to infiltrate the mind. Do not confuse this with reading minds. Demonic spirits do not possess the ability to read minds. What they can do is project images and cast dreams to a person. They have the power to incite the flesh into lustful desires. When a person is not satisfied in their spirit, the desire for satisfaction is met by entities that are not of this world. They begin to satisfy the desires of the person's flesh through dreams and emotions.

Incubus

Now you might ask, why am I talking about these types of spirits when talking about marriage? Well, let's first define what is an incubus spirit. An incubus spirit is a spirit that typically climbs on top of a woman and either attempts to have sex with her or arouse her at night. With the woman, it's more emotional in their approach.

Succubus

A succubus spirit is a spirit that comes after a man. Usually they come in the form of dreams. The man will dream that he is having sex with a woman. It will feel real and lifelike. The goal is to cause the man to ejaculate. In the ejaculation is oftentimes the point of orgasm for the man. That is when is it easiest to get to the emotional aspect of the man.

Wet dreams

A wet dream is when a person is dreaming that they are having a sexual encounter. They will feel that it is an actual situation. This dream usually will cause guilt and shame at the point of waking up.

The guilt and shame is designed to keep you quiet, to keep an open door to you. These spirits only want an open door to your life to keep you struggling with the flesh.

Sexually weakening spirits

These spirits are the same type that operated in Samson's life. They knew they couldn't defeat Samson militarily, physically, or even outsmart him, so they went after his weakness. His lust was what was visible, but his pride and vainglory was at the center of his heart. This was living in the center of his heart, and the enemy knew it. His lust for foreign women was apparent. So the enemy came to give him what he desired. Yes, the enemy provides good fleshly gifts. He provides what the flesh desires in order to capture your heart.

"But each person is tempted when they are dragged away by their own evil desire and enticed." (James 1:14 NIV).

As I mentioned earlier in the chapter, the enemy is able to see what is going on through the windows we open, which is our behavior. So depending on what you're acting like, he will be able to see what he can use against you and your marriage. Samson could have easily stopped the enemy's advancement against him by simply humbling himself to God and listening to his parents.

Humility and worship are the most powerful weapons against vanity and pride. It makes you recognize that there is one higher than you and that what you have was not you that acquired it on your own but him that gave it to you. I remember being on vacation with my wife for her birthday. I told her I had to use the restroom. When I entered the restroom, the Holy Spirit deposited a thought in my mind. You know, those moments the Holy Spirit drops thoughts to lead you down a thought process to bring you to a conclusion on a matter?

Well, this time, he spoke to me about Samson, how he gave so much ability to Samson. He began to let me know that those that have been given so much from God have to constantly be in a state of humility and worship. Pride and vanity makes you want to stand up and put yourself on display as if whatever was done was done because of you. It makes you rob God of his glory. God will never share his glory with anyone.

"I am the Lord; that is my name! I will not yield my glory to another or my praise to idols" (Isaiah 42:8 NIV).

Humility and worship are amazing weapons against this. Humility works against pride. Pride makes you feel better than the next person because of how good you are. Humility makes you feel undeserving. It makes you feel like others are more important and that you need to make way for them in place of you. That keeps pride down. Here are some verses for you to see how humility works:

"Humble yourselves, therefore, under God's mighty hand, that he may lift you up in due time" (1 Peter 5:6 NIV).

"But he gives us more grace. That is why Scripture says: 'God opposes the proud but shows favor to the humble'" (James 4:6 NIV).

"Humble yourselves before the Lord, and he will lift you up" (James 4:10 NIV).

"When pride comes, then comes disgrace, but with humility comes wisdom" (Proverbs 11:2 NIV).

Worship works against vanity. Vanity makes you look at yourself as a god. It makes you receive the praises of the people for your splendor and accolades. It keeps you from saying all glory goes to God. Worship makes you recognize that what you got came from God and God alone, and that you have him as your higher power. It keeps you in a constant state of fear to the Lord. Here are some verses to illustrate how worship works:

"Worship the Lord your God, and his blessing will be on your food and water. I will take away sickness from among you" (Exodus 23:25 NIV).

"For from him and through him and for him are all things. To him be the glory forever! Amen" (Romans 11:36 NIV).

"He is the one you praise; he is your God, who performed for you those great and awesome wonders you saw with your own eyes" (Deuteronomy 10:21 NIV).

Samson's struggle with lust after non-Hebrew women revealed that he loved the world. The kingdom of darkness allowed him to win public victories, but his private struggle was where the real battle took place. The devil managed to get someone to get too close for comfort.

Delilah was able to please him sexually and get the secret of his strength. His dangerous game with sin managed to debilitate him. This is a satanic plan. It is designed to debilitate ministers and Christians. The enemy is okay with you winning certain battles, so long as he can defeat you in private. It is in those private moments where we will be looked at intensely at the day of judgment.

It was all happening to me

You might ask why I am talking about all of these thing. Because, sadly enough, this was all happening to me in my marriage. I was experiencing all that I mentioned. I was battling in these areas in my life, and I didn't know how deep the enemy was in my life. I was allowing the public victories and awesome battles that I was over-coming as a badge of honor. But deep from within, I was drowning. I was a religious person. I was more in love with the ritualistic aspect of my servitude than a relationship with God. My eyes were wander-ing more and more after other women. I, like Samson, couldn't stop looking at foreign women. I was looking at other women, rather than just being satisfied and happy with my wife. That, coupled with the porn addiction, I had myself a slow-moving storm brewing in the troubled waters of my heart.

Now I know I will get flak for this, but being in a real com-mitted relationship is hard work. I know the theology police will come after me (I kid...) because they say it's not about works. But it's the truth. There are a ton of scriptural references in the Old and in the New Testament that point to what we ought to do once we are in Christ. Contrary to what many people believe, God doesn't do everything for us. There are commands that he expects us to do. He has given us grace and power to be able to execute tasks and achieve goals that we set for ourselves in order for us to stay in the path of righteousness.

So to be ritualistic, rather than relational, we have no reason to truly keep the Word of the Lord in our hearts. As long as we do the rituals, we will be okay; and that is one of the greatest lies the enemy is telling the church. This was me. My wife was held hostage to my lack of desire for a true relationship with the Lord.

Emissarial visitation

The year was 2011, and I was so weak spiritually. I had a dream where I was in my bedroom, and I heard a commotion in the living room. I got up and went to check. As I opened the door of my bedroom, I walked into the living room, and I saw a very large and tall man. This was not a regular man. He was about seven and a half feet tall. He was very large (heavyset). He wasn't sloppy looking. He looked like one of the world's strong man competitors. As I was standing there, looking at this being, he turned and looked back at me. As he was looking back at me, I saw him dressed in all black, wearing a face mask and hood, almost like a ninja or an Arab fighter—best way for me to describe him. I could see his eyes. I saw the whites of his eyes, but his pupils where red. I could tell this thing wasn't human. The skin around his eyes and face looked almost reptilelike and leathery. He was holding a large sack behind him as a thief carrying and running off with the loot.

Oftentimes, in these spiritual vision dreams, a person will know things that will otherwise be unknown in the natural realm. You will just know things. When in the spirit realm, and/or spirit form, you will have knowledge of things without even knowing how. An example of this is how when you are dreaming with someone, and you don't see the person, but you know it's them. In my dream, I knew that this was a satanic emissary sent from the dark realm and kingdom to spy on me.

I could tell he stole something from me. As I went forward to catch him, he walked to the wall, and it opened up like a portal. I ran to get him, and he jumped through it. When I came out of the dream/vision, I knew he stole strength from me. God was showing me that the enemy was working at covertly weakening me, and I was not doing anything to stop him. This is where things go overboard, and I cross the line.

8

The Line Was Crossed

My flesh was so unsatisfied that porn and masturbation was not enough. At this point, the desire for sexual satisfaction was very difficult to hide. Uninhibited flirtation was the norm. I know this may sound like a shock to many, especially to those that know me, but this is my truth. What makes this even more shocking is that many preachers, married preachers, and Christians go through this. The amount of unacceptable behavior within the body of Christ is shocking.

My marriage was at an all-time low. The constant fighting and regret for one another was now noticeable. We would have church leaders at our home to stop us from fighting. My pastor and other leaders would show up to referee our arguments. It was bad. My wife hated me, and I hated her. It's so horrible to even say it now and admit that. But when God is not at the center of your relationship, what else can you expect?

I could no longer hide my battle with the flesh from my wife. She once walked into the room as I viewed porn on the computer. I did what most people do when watching it. I shut the monitor off and asked if I could help her. It was embarrassing and still is to think about. Unfortunately, this is very common among preachers and pastors. It just so happens that many do not talk about it.

Self-delusion

I was now preaching more, and now I was known among the "inner-church circle." So many more people were starting to notice me as a preacher, especially the women. I would see how they would look at me as I would walk into a church building. I could almost tell every single time when someone looked at me a certain way. It is a look that your flesh reacts to. It's not only women that do it but men as well. It is a look that creates self-delusion. It is designed to make you think that you are the best-looking guy in the room. It is designed to stroke your ego. It is designed to make you plunge into a delusional reality that only you live in.

The enemy knows that you are weak. He knows your defenses are down. He can see an opening. This is when he launches his attack. For so long, what he has been doing was feeding you a false reality. The devil does not need you to do many sins. He just wants and needs you to do at least one sin but do it repeatedly. Sinning repeatedly causes the heart to be calloused. Having a calloused heart causes the believer to lose the fear of the Lord, and that is exactly what happened to me.

One thing I know now that I didn't know then is that if you play with fire, you will eventually most certainly burn. I kept feeding my flesh. Constantly feeding your flesh will 100 percent end in destruction. I thought that because I was not having sex with anyone that it wouldn't escalate. My heart was calloused. I kept doing one sin and doing it repeatedly. I lost the fear that kept me in the holiness of God. Now before you start to say we shouldn't be afraid of God, let me tell you that biblical fear of God is not the same as the spirit of fear.

This fear is respect. This fear is reverence. This fear is to know that he is greater than us, and that at any moment, he can end us with ease. Jesus says that we are not to fear he that can destroy the body but fear the one that can destroy the body and the soul in hell. It is a righteous fear that comes upon every true born-again believer that has a true encounter with the Lord. When you are in relationship with someone, you fear cheating on them because of the love you have for that person. This is the same fear that made Joseph run almost completely naked from Potiphar's wife. That is what happens when you are in relationship with the Eternal One.

My first love

I lost the fear of the Lord. But why? How could this have happened? You might say I never had it with still being bound to porn and lust. But I had enough fear to keep me from jumping off the deep end. You see, there were many youth that I started with in church that would just lay down and fornicate. But I knew better and had enough sense than to do that. I knew that if I did that, it would open a door that I feared would never close or be nearly impossible to close.

Closing an open door that is attached to the heart is so much harder to close than a door that is not. In other words, emotional doors are almost impossible to close. Without God, it is not possible. He is the one that opens doors that no one can shut, and he is the one that shuts doors that no one can open.

"I will place on his shoulder the key to the house of David; what he opens no one can shut, and what he shuts no one can open" (Isaiah 22:22 NIV).

But I did what most do now and days. I read the Word for ministerial opportunities, rather than it being for self-transformational purposes. I wasn't being transformed because I was not applying the Word. So not knowing the Word correctly kept me from understanding that sin never stays in its initial state. Sin grows. Sin's desire is to multiply. I referenced this verse in an earlier chapter, but it perfectly illustrates what I am saying.

"Then, after desire has conceived, it gives birth to sin; and sin, when it is full-grown, gives birth to death" (James 1:15 NIV).

The desire and lust in my heart grew to a point that I could no longer contain it. Two years into my marriage, and I was now higher in ministry. I got signed to a small independent record label to record my first record. I had my life planned out. I put God in a box, expecting him to do according to the plans that I had made for myself. Notice I said for myself because I didn't take my wife's feelings and desires into consideration.

Satanic activation

Since I was advancing in the ministry, I was also hearing from God more. Despite my spiritual condition, God still had plans. God endeavored in doing all that he planned for me since the beginning. God already knew what I was going to go through since before time began, before he ever said, "Let there be light." When preachers would come to minister to my local church, they would minister to me the words of the Lord. I would get directions and instructions from God.

But just like that, the enemy was lurking and ready to activate his plan he had for my life. He crafted his plan since my birth. Satan and his cohorts study and conduct their own trial-and-error runs on humans. They try many things to see what you bite on. Mine happened to be lust. This started as I would go out to minister. I would go and sing before preaching and saw how the ladies would react to my talent. One thing I learned is that many women love a talented man in authority. I would see how they would look at me. I would see how their eyes were stuck on me as if to give off a signal.

I realized that when I got married, it intensified. The unattainable is more attractive and desirable. It is what we cannot and should not have that the flesh desires most. So it was at this junction of my ministerial career that Satan began to activate the sleeper cells. He activated those that would serve as what he masterfully prepared to be my fall. I am by no means praising him or giving him glory. But I am not ignoring his schemes. The Bible tells us not to ignore the devil's schemes.

"In order that Satan might not outwit us. For we are not unaware of his schemes" (2 Corinthians 2:11 NIV).

I remember a service where I went to preach. As I preached, I saw a certain female that would ever so often lock eyes with me. She looked at me as I sang before I delivered the message that night. I knew she wanted me. Her piercing and intense glances were enough to interfere with my connection with God as I performed before the congregation. It was very difficult to concentrate as her eyes were puffing up my ego. Satan had his people in the crowd. For those who believe that demonic spirits do not attend our services, I have news for you, they do, and they do often.

"In the synagogue there was a man possessed by a demon, an impure spirit. He cried out at the top of his voice" (Luke 4:33 NIV).

Sleeper cells

He activated this female to trigger the lust he knew was inside me. It wasn't just church. He had covert servants in many places I went to. It was everywhere. When he saw me get close to the Spirit of God, he would activate something or someone. He didn't care that I went to church. Satan is okay with you being religious. In fact, he loves religious people the most because, outside, religious people look like God, but inside, they look like him. Through them, he has the ability to be inside the crowd that serves the Lord. He can even be in the inner circle of the congregation. This is his tactic from the beginning. I was one of them.

"One day the angels came to present themselves before the Lord, and Satan also came with them" (Job 1:6 NIV).

You see, the kingdom of darkness desires to infiltrate the very courts of God. He desires to invade everything that is of God. This is spoken of in the Old Testament, in the book of *Isaiah 14:13–14. The prophet Isaiah says:*

> You said in your heart, "I will ascend to the heavens; I will raise my throne above the stars of God; I will sit enthroned on the mount of assembly, on the utmost heights of Mount Zaphon. I will ascend above the tops of the clouds; I will make myself like the Most High."

He desires to be the god of the disobedient. He desires to be the god of those who doubt the Word of the Lord deep in their hearts.

So he will allow them to reach certain levels in the Gospel, but he will allow it religiously. Satan has many sleeping agents in this world, especially within the church. This same situation happened in the Bible, in Joshua, chapter 9, with the Gibeonite deception. They came disguised as innocent people. They were able to fool Joshua and the Israelite leaders. Satan's tactics are still the same. This is one of the ways he manages to overtake and destroy many pastors and laymen in the church of Jesus Christ.

There was a shift

It was around this time that my local church was going through a transition. It was going through a church split. The perpetrators that spearheaded the attempted coup left a lot of damage in the church. It managed to shift the atmosphere and culture of the church. Things that were once a no-no became okay to do. Not all things, but some things; and that's all the enemy needs. All he needs is a little opening, and he has his way in. There's an old saying, "Give the devil an inch, and he'll take a mile." Oh, how true that phrase is. One of the most dangerous things you could do is to leave an opening unattended. This is where the wolves come in.

A willing victim

As the church was still going through the healing process, I was still hiding all of what I was and had inside my heart. There was a certain young lady that came new to the church. She was fresh into the Gospel. I never paid any attention to her as I knew better than to mess with someone the Lord was rescuing. Time went on, and we became friends; nothing more, nothing less. Because of circumstances that were out of everyone's control, we were forced to work together in the church.

We were given the charge of running certain departments and tasks in the church. We grew closer together and became better friends. I was going through the motions of a failed marriage. She was going through the healing process of her past. We began to do the logical thing: confide in each other. We began to tell each other how we were feeling in life. I did what most spouses do when they open the door to adultery: confess to the wrong person. I made myself look like a victim to her. I never took responsibility for my actions and decisions in my marriage. I blamed my wife for all the bad that was happening in my marriage. I made myself look like a saint. I became more than a victim. I became a willing victim. Willing victims are those who allow themselves to be abused because they find a sense of pleasure and security in the coddling that follows.

The enemy lends an ear

I began to tell her things that I should have been taking to my pastor and to God in prayer. This is what many people do. Because their prayer life is nonexistent, they look for the next best thing. They look for someone that can tickle their ear with the answers they want to hear. And if that is what you want, the enemy is right there to lend an ear. He will provide people to listen to you. He will place people right by your side for you to spill the beans on the secrets of your strength. Remember what I said about Samson in the previous chapter? Well, this is how it looks. Now I don't want to just paint the picture that it was just her doing the listening and being used by the enemy. I, too, was listening. I, too, was being used by the enemy to destroy her.

Collateral damage

As harsh as that sounds and as shameful as it sounds, it's the truth. I was also being used by the enemy to destroy this young lady's life. She, too, was a soul of salvation. She, too, had been prophesied to by God that God was going to use her. The enemy was trying to destroy us both. Not only did he plan on destroying us both, but he was banking on the collateral damage that would happen due to the fallout of the scandal if he could get the situation to that point. As the time progressed, so did our relationship.

Priming the pump

Three years have gone by that she was at the church, and three years that we have been friends. Our friendship grew closer and closer. You might ask where was my wife in all this? Well, she was there. The enemy was working on her as well. She was having so many issues in her prayer life and in our relationship that she was an emotional wreck. There was an incident at the church with one of the leaders that really hurt my wife. I know that no one can stop you from going to church.

The Word of God says in Romans 8:38–39 (NIV):

> For I am convinced that neither death nor life, neither angels nor demons, neither the present nor the future, nor any powers, neither height nor depth, nor anything else in all creation, will be able to separate us from the love of God that is in Christ Jesus our Lord.

I am well aware that no one can keep us away from God's love but, looking back, I also know that Satan was priming the pump in this situation.

God reveals through dreams with symbolism

The enemy of the souls was setting up the situation for there to be a fall from grace. He was setting up all of the necessary components to trap every participant involved. I remember waking from a dream where I saw a huge spider come down. I saw it in front of me. I don't remember seeing where I was or what was around me. I just remember seeing this spider almost like a tarantula. It was abnormally bigger than a normal tarantula. More than its size, I remember noticing the color spots on the legs. They were pink. Normally, you see a tarantula, and it would be either black or dark brown with light brown spots on its legs.

This particular spider was black with pink on the legs. It was on a huge web that it weaved. I struggled to truly understand the meaning of this dream, so I went to my pastor. I told my pastor the dream, and he looked me right in the eyes and said there was a woman that the enemy was going to use to destroy me and trap me. He then said that the woman might not even know she was going to be used. What he didn't know was that there was a woman already interwoven in my life. The enemy was weaving his web of deception and death to trap us both.

God will always warn you before something happens. God is a good God that is truly looking out for your best interest. Being the God that he is, he will do whatever it takes to make this happen. Part of what he does is reveals it to people and to you, using various ways and methods.

- *He will reveal it to his prophets.* *"Surely the Sovereign Lord does nothing without revealing his plan to his servants the prophets" (Amos 3:7 NIV).* You can see this example in the old testament when King David committed adultery with Bathsheba and then murdered her husband to cover the sin. The prophet Nathan came to him and confronted him about what he did.

- *He will reveal it through dreams.* *"And afterward, I will pour out my Spirit on all people. Your sons and daughters will prophesy, your old men will dream dreams, your young men will see visions" (Joel 2:28 NIV).* This was confirmed in Acts 2:2–3, when the Holy Spirit came into the upper room. The apostle Peter stood up and explained that what was happening was the fulfillment of the prophet Joel. This activated the church to be able to see in the spirit realm and receive from God supernaturally without a prophet.

- *He will give visions.* Just like dreams, visions are images given in the mind while awake. The difference between dreams and visions is that dreams are night visions that you see when you are sleeping. Your subconscious is able to receive from God without distraction. That's why, oftentimes, dreams are more vivid and full of detail and seemingly longer. In that same way, visions are essentially daydreams.

God warned me and warned me, but I was so sold on the idea of feeding my flesh and indulging in my desire that I did not heed to the warnings. There was a Sunday while at church at my local church, when one of the ladies of the church approached me. I and this lady didn't really get along. I was sitting in the pastor's office when she walked in. She pulled a chair and said, "God bless you, brother. I need to talk to you."

I said to her, "Amen. God bless you as well. What do you want to talk about?"

She began to tell me that God told her to go to me to tell me to be careful.

When I asked her what I was to be careful about, she told me the female's name who I was talking to secretly. As soon as she told me, my pride was in full display. I began to tell her why she needs to tell me that when I wasn't doing anything. She said, "I don't know what is happening. I just know that what God told me to say to you."

I started to tell her that I knew what I was doing and that I wasn't going to fall. And, boy, was I wrong. I was telling her these things, while deep inside my heart, I was already lusting over this particular female.

As the situation progressed between the female and I, God would keep speaking to both her and I. In retrospect, I strongly believe that God did everything to get our attention in attempts to walk us back from the ledge and taking the plunge into a life of despair, pain, and separation from him. God was also speaking to her. I didn't know it at the time because I was so consumed with myself that I never took the time to see that she, too, was someone that God wanted to save.

Satanic opportunities

The entire time God was trying to stop us from falling, the devil was truly trying on his end to derail us. Every twist and turn we took, the enemy of the souls set up opportunities for us to be alone together, all to fuel the lust and vulnerability we both were feeling in our hearts. The enemy takes advantage of the lowly. They love to push humans into unfavorable situations to distort reality to the point where they believe the lies presented to them.

Sin is fuel

The kingdom of darkness is fueled by the sin of humanity. The Bible says when Jesus is speaking about the parable of the strong man, he talks about the fact that you cannot enter and plunder the strong man's house without binding him. The question that rises when I read that parable is this one: How did that strong man become the strong man of that house? Well, first he had to have some type of access. He has built himself a fortified safe haven in the home.

The kingdom of darkness operates the same way. The spiritual realm works and operates by legalities. They can only operate and be where there is sin and no presence of God. Saying no presence of God is oxymoronic, to say the least, because God is omnipresent. But when I say where there is no presence of God, it is places where God is not worshipped. Jesus speaks of this.

"When an impure spirit comes out of a person, it goes through arid places seeking rest and does not find it" (Matthew 12:43 NIV).

Jesus is explaining how the process of demonic possession takes place. When the unclean spirit is cast out of a heart, it goes out to arid places. Other versions refer to this as waterless or dry places. These are places and people where God is not worshipped. Demonic spirits have legal right to be there because God is not the God of that place, person, or nation. The more sinful, the more authority the kingdom of darkness has. Throughout my pastoral career, I have encountered many demonic liberations, and almost every time, I have heard the demon tell me how they got in. It was never because of doing something righteous.

Satan was grabbing a foothold on our situation. He was becoming stronger and more powerful in our lives, with the ability to influence and entice us to sin. It was all because there was no presence of

God in our situation. In the book of Zechariah 3:1–3, we see what was taking place in the spirit realm.

> Then he showed me Joshua the high priest standing before the angel of the Lord, and Satan standing at his right side to accuse him. The Lord said to Satan, "The Lord rebuke you, Satan! The Lord, who has chosen Jerusalem, rebuke you! Is not this man a burning stick snatched from the fire?" Now Joshua was dressed in filthy clothes as he stood before the angel. (Zechariah 3:1–3 NIV)

The line was crossed

With the stronghold of the enemy in both our lives, this female and I were en route to step over the ledge. On one particular day, my wife was at work, and I was home. Since I had no prayer life, I had time to waste. That was so dangerous. I was living full-time ministry, so I lived doing ministry all day, every day. The female messaged me early in the morning as she was accustomed to doing. She and I would message and call each other every morning, afternoon, and night. We nurtured a relationship without even trying. Many people don't understand how the growth of a relationship happens. It happens when two people spend more time with each other.

This same concept can and should be applied to our relationship with God. This is what we should have been doing. If we would have spent more time in the presence of God, things would have been so much better. But on this day, things went south. She sent me a message early, right after my wife went to work. She asked me to go over to her home. Of course, I was scared, nervous but also excited. I wanted to. You see, the devil will never present you with something you do not like. He can try, but it will not work. He will entice you with what you love, and at this point, I wanted it and was in love with the idea.

I said yes to going to her home that morning. I said yes to being selfish. I said yes to taking the plunge and the fall from grace as they say. I went that morning and met her at home. I walked in and felt the Holy Spirit saying no. I felt the words of the Bible screaming at me as I walked into her home. I knew I should not have done it, but the fleshly desire was so strong, and my proclivity to experience worldliness was at its highest. Not only was my flesh a driving force, but the pain of my failed marriage and my desire to refuge myself in this female's presence that I gave myself over to sin.

The relationship progressed, and I was drifting further and further from the presence of God. The line was not only crossed, but it was now miles away, to the point that both she and I could no longer see it. I wasn't just the only one that was in this. She was also drifting further away from the Lord. I was now in adultery. I cheated. I did what I always told myself I wouldn't. I didn't know how to deal with it. I did the first thing that came to mind, and that was to hide it.

Hide in the bushes

The guilt and shame was strong that I didn't know how to handle what I just did. I was so afraid to confess this as I knew that the condemnation was going to be so great. I knew that a scandal was what many people wanted. So I hid. I hid in the bushes, just like Adam and Eve did. I spoke about Adam and Eve in chapter 5, but when Adam and Eve heard that God was in the garden, looking for them, they hid in the bushes or trees. The bushes or trees represent religiosity. After God called them out from where they were hiding, both Adam and Eve came out wearing fig leaves. Prophetically, fig trees represent Israel. Now in this case, Adam and Eve had sewn fig-leaf coverings for themselves to cover their nakedness and shame before the Lord.

In the same way that Israel is trying to hold on to their own righteousness without Christ, Adam and Eve did so religiously. They attempted to cover their sin with their own righteousness. We know that the only thing that can cover our sin is the blood of Christ. The

Bible teaches that there is no forgiveness of sin without the shedding of blood of a perfect sacrifice.

"In fact, the law requires that nearly everything be cleansed with blood, and without the shedding of blood there is no forgiveness" (Hebrews 9:22 NIV).

So I myself hid and used figs. I wrapped myself in religiosity, all so that no one would know what I did. I continued to minister in this condition. I would go to churches knowing that I was actively in adultery. I am sure that many, upon reading this, will have many questions. Many, perhaps, will ask how it was possible for me to continue to preach. Many will ask if I was afraid. The answer is yes, I was afraid. In fact, I was terrified. I was so afraid that I started to excuse myself from church. I started to even lie and say that I was going to a church to minister when, in fact, I was not.

I kept this charade up for as long as I could. The female did the same. Since I was in church longer than her, I felt the effects of the Word of God when it was preached. I would sit in the congregation while my pastor was being used by God to deliver powerful convicting messages that would make the most hardened sinners turn their hearts to God upon hearing it. My heart became so calloused that I would not think about the consequences. Although I was terrified, I was so trapped and into the sin.

Loving the sin

I fell in love with the sin! I couldn't stay away from this girl. I not only fell with her, but I gave my heart into the situation. You see, sinning is one thing, but when the heart gets involved, it takes the situation to a whole other situation. We both convinced ourselves that we were in love with each other. There were nights when after being together, we would feel so much remorse over what we were doing that we would pray and ask God to help us to get out of the situation.

Free will

I, like many, used to believe that when someone comes to God and accepts him that he automatically sets them free. I have learned that's not true. God does not violate someone's free will. He will never get in the way of someone's choice. God loves us so much that he does not force his creation to serve him. Some people just simply have not given up their love for the sin that they do. For you to be set free, you have to truly desire to be free. God uses the prophet Jeremiah to say it like this: *"You will seek me and find me when you seek me with all your heart" (Jeremiah 29:13 NIV).*

There cannot be anything left in the heart. When on the road to being set free, you have to be absolutely tired. You have to hate what God hates. You have to give God every single part of your heart. This is why some things take time to be set free from. God has to walk us through some things over time. That's why we both would pray, and nothing would happen. Yes, we wanted to be free, but we still loved what we were doing and loved the codependency we had on each other.

This went on until I couldn't hide it anymore. Months into the now full-blown adultery, I could no longer hear the messages and stand the guilt. I started to miss church services more and more. I started to even lie to the churches that invited me to go minister at their services. The guilt was so present. I remember going to a service in Philadelphia, where God used the preacher to anonymously call out our situation. God saw everything that was happening.

One service missed turned into two. Two turned to five, and five turned to two weeks. It progressed to the point where I was now three months out of church. One morning, my pastor came to my home to speak to me. I was so afraid to open the door. I just peeked through the window like a coward. I couldn't face him. I was so afraid of the guilt, shame, and scandal that would ensue. Time passed by, and I was officially backslidden. I was now out of church and out of a relationship with God. The sister I was involved with stayed. She had to or else the entire thing would unravel. Many nights, I spent in fear, sadness, loneliness, and depression.

The Holy Spirit would visit me at night and desire to have communion with me, and I would just turn over in my bed and ask him to leave me alone. I couldn't stand how I felt. I desired to be free of the situation I was in. Both the female and I desired to be free but just didn't know how to bring ourselves to do it. You see, the enemy was binding us in our minds, trying to make us believe that by leaving the situation, we would hurt the other. This continued a few years. God had mercy because he could have let me die in my sin. But he loved me enough to have mercy. God is so merciful that even in a situation like this, God pours out his grace and mercy.

9

The Church and Her Secrets

This chapter is not easy to write. It is very difficult to talk about. But it is a reality that many choose to ignore. The church of Jesus Christ has secrets! The design of the church is one that encourages confession, and through confession, we have an escape from the things that grip us and keep us bound to things that live in darkness. One of the most ironic things you can do is to be a part of an organism that lives in the light of the Lord and run from that light and abide in darkness by hiding sin.

One thing that doesn't shock me as much anymore, but still has an effect on me, is the blatant disregard for holiness among the ministerial body of Jesus Christ. I am not ignorant to the fact that it happens. But when I see someone that is on the altar, being used by the Lord, and then later find out that he or she is living a double life, it still amazes me how there are those who dare straddle the fence between light and darkness. I am not as shocked as I have done the same. That's why this book was written, to bring light into the dark places that live in the church of Jesus Christ.

Discernment

In my most humble opinion, the most important gift of the Holy Spirit to the church is the gift of discernment. The gift of discernment is one of the most talked about gifts among many ministerial circles as of late, but few ministers and churches are able to prove they have it or operate in it. Discernment is so crucial for having a healthy, functioning altar and congregation. It allows you to be aware of what is happening in the unseen realm. If you're into comic book superheroes like I am, you'll see it as Spiderman's spider sense or Spidey-Sense. Of course, I am not saying that the discernment is a superhero power, but it works in the same way.

The Holy Spirit will alert you intuitively that something is not right or will make you feel the truth about a situation, person, and/or persons. This is so important because we are living in an era where everyone says that they are believers. Before, it was easy to distinguish between a believer and a nonbeliever as women wouldn't wear pants, and men wore suits all the time. Yes, this was the culture in the United States in the fifties and sixties, but the church adopted the look to differentiate between the world and itself. So it was easy to know who was who. But today, most of the church has done away with almost all dogmas. So now there is virtually no difference between believers and nonbelievers outwardly.

This situation was also happening in the New Testament. In the letter written by the apostle Jude, also known as Thaddeus, who was one of the original disciples of Jesus Christ, he felt compelled to write that there were some men that crept in secretly among the believers. Saint Jude says that they were ungodly men. How were they able to infiltrate the community of believers? Well, It wasn't by looking culturally different. It was by looking, speaking, and living exactly like the believers. But once the Holy Spirit started to alert the church, they were able to identify those that were covertly imbedded among the church.

"For certain individuals whose condemnation was written about long ago have secretly slipped in among you. They are ungodly people, who pervert the grace of our God into a license for immorality and deny Jesus Christ our only Sovereign and Lord" (Jude 1:4 NIV).

They were able to identify with the discernment of the Holy Spirit. The Holy Spirit isn't always going to show you with detail everything that is happening behind the scenes about something. But oftentimes, he will alert you in your spirit through the gift of discernment. This is one of the gifts that many people say they have but usually don't. Why do I say they usually don't have it? Because if all the people that say that they have it actually had it, we wouldn't see as much chaos and scandals that we do in the church today.

Where has the discernment gone?

I have been asked this question many times in my ministerial career. I would dare say that many of the questions that get asked all come from the same place: confusion. People often hear how God cannot use someone who is actively in sin, but the truth of the matter is that he can and he does. I am not advocating for us to continue in sin and allowing God to use us. I am saying that I, like many other ministerial colleagues of mine, have been shocked when we see God using someone we deem not fit to minister or preach the Word of God.

So the question remains, where has the discernment gone? Can we say that God no longer reveals? Is it safe to say that God no longer activates discernment in the people? Absolutely not! God still does everything he did in the early church. The problem is that the church has a problem with flirting with the world. The church tends, from time to time, to lie down with the world. God is holy. He moves in a holy atmosphere. There has to be a fertile atmosphere for God to begin to move among the people.

Connection

There has to be a connection to the divine revelation of God. There has to be someone that can connect to the vision of God. Holiness is the key. Holiness allows God to move because there is an absence of the world. James tells us that being a friend of the world makes us an enemy of God, and we know that God does not share his secrets with his enemies.

"You adulterous people, don't you know that friendship with the world means enmity against God? Therefore, anyone who chooses to be a friend of the world becomes an enemy of God" (James 4:4 NIV).

Discernment can literally uncover plans that are moving in the background. Discernment is crucial for properly reading and measuring the atmosphere to know what God intends for that particular moment. It also gives you the ability to tell the wolves from the sheep. With such a great portion of the church being so preoccupied with social media, vanity, and fame, there has been a neglect to the things of the Lord, so much so that many, like Jude says, have crept in unaware, and because of this, scandals like never before have risen from within the church. I don't want to paint the picture that there is no one that is connected to God, but I am saying that there is a great absence in the church for men and women who want to stand for truth, righteousness, and in the light of God.

The patriarchal anointing

In my years of ministering, I have heard some crazy and outlandish stories of men and women in the Gospel. I have heard of adulteries, fornications and, believe it or not, money laundering by ministers. But one of the most shocking things that I heard and was made aware of was "the patriarchal anointing." Now I certainly did not intend this chapter and this book, even as a source of gossip, which I'm sure that there are going to be those that will think so. But my reason for this book and this chapter, in particular, is to shed light on what is moving in the background so that you can have a clear understanding of what the church is facing.

Early in the ministry, when I began to travel, I made many friends along the way. I would meet people who were awesome at what they did and how they ministered for the Lord. Of course, when you meet them, they begin to open up about their experiences and knowledge they have obtained in the ministry. One of those friends is a dear friend of mine I met in Florida as I was traveling. He began to tell me about something he was offered in one of his trips. He began to explain to me that after a service in one the churches he went to preach at, he was approached by the pastor of the church and was asked if he had any needs.

My friend, of course, not thinking anything wrong, said, "No, I'm fine." He tells the pastor, "I already ate, and there's water in the fridge back in the hotel room. Thank you."

The pastor looks at him and smiles and says, "No, my brother, I mean do you have any needs?" As he is saying this, he looks at one of the young girls that was standing in the church, talking. He was offering him a young teenage girl for him to have his way with back at his hotel room, to satisfy his sexual needs.

Now you can see my bewilderment upon hearing this. This is a demonically twisted and distorted take on the ancient patriarchal rules where the patriarchal leaders had the right to sleep with any of the women of the tribe. This happens among some churches and is most certainly not biblical. God does not do this. In fact, the Word of God tells us that sex is to be between one man and one woman in holy matrimony. We can see the perversion and sexually deviant mindset settling in, quietly disguised as a biblically established principle.

G12

Several years ago, there was a movement moving in the church, especially the Hispanic church, called "G12 Vision" or also known as "the Encounter." It was started in Columbia by a man named César Castellanos. César Castellanos is a neocharismatic pastor from Bogotá, Colombia, and the founder of the Misión Carismática Internacional. Castellanos is known as the leading proponent of the G12 Vision, which is based upon the mentoring of twelve disciples. This movement caught on all over. Here in the US, many churches were following the G12 pattern.

After about a year after it caught on here in the States, there were rumors that started to travel around the churches that there was sexual misconduct happening in the secret meetings they called the Encounter. I didn't know much about it until it was brought to my attention one day. There was a woman named Ambar Diaz. Ambar was married to one of the higher officials of this movement. She testifies of the sinful things that would take place in their meetings called "Encounters." She tells of how the G12 movement was on a mission to destroy churches that did not want to join their ranks. She speaks of the sexual assaults that would take place in these meetings.

These things took place under the noses of many believers. They took place under the disguise of a new vision within the body of Jesus Christ. The shocking thing about this is the amount of pastors and their churches that went along with this heretical movement without vetting it and holding it against the Word of God to see if it was theologically correct. Because of the cunning wit and craftiness of many ungodly men, many people have gone astray, going after doctrines of demons.

LGBTQ on the altar

For years, the church has stood against homosexuality. For years, the church has condemned homosexuality. But for years, the church had men and women that had straddled the fence they publicly preached against. It's always shocking to hear when someone is found to be in sin. Especially those sins that are sexually immoral, theft, and/or domestic violence. But when they are sins the person stands on the pulpit and preaches against, it's even more shocking.

Such is the case when we hear of preachers who preach hard against homosexuality and then are later found to be involved in the same sin. This has happened many times over. Unfortunately, this has happened one too many times, and when it does, it still has the same effect when the news breaks. Many people and ministers in the church forget that although we are in the Lord, although we are covered and anointed, we are still human, susceptible to falling in sin. This flesh is still attracted to what the world has to offer.

There have been men and women who preach so hard against homosexuality and later are found to have been in involved sexually with someone of the same sex all along. A few years ago, there was a prominent well-known preacher who was caught in a sexual scandal with a few young men. He was a pastor with a large church based out of Atlanta. There was a group of young men who were accusing the pastor of having sexual relations with them. There were compromising photos sent to them from the pastor.

This was shocking because the pastor would preach against homosexuality and stood for biblical righteousness. Once the scandal broke, there were young men coming forward, accusing the pastor of sexual misconduct. The pastor denied it, of course. But the lawsuits came, and the truth began to come out, little by little. The pastor was left in shame, and exposure started to set in. The exposure began to shine a light on the fact that, although the church preaches against homosexuality, it isn't exempt from having some of its ministers secretly living out this lifestyle while operating in the ministerial body.

I am not writing this to make homosexuality worse than any other sin, but I am saying that we cannot be ignorant and naive to think that this isn't something that isn't happening in many churches in America and the world. The church has to accept the idea that men and women of God are not god. We have deified men and women of God. Although there are levels and platforms that God has given them, many people are holding them up to levels and platforms that were never meant for them, then drop them like trash when they fail and fall, when their humanity steps in the way.

In the past, the LGBTQ had no voice when it came to the church. There was a major consensus within the church, and that consensus was that homosexuality was a sin. It is clearly stated in the Bible that it is. "Or do you not know that wrongdoers will not inherit the kingdom of God? Do not be deceived: Neither the sexually immoral nor idolaters nor adulterers nor men who have sex with men" (1 Corinthians 6:9 NIV). But due to the church becoming more like the world and less like Christ, we see a weakening of the guard. We see how the defenses are down.

Now we have sympathizers, instead of men and women with conviction. We have entered the age of conformity. The church is full of conformers. Yes, I realize that this sounds like I am condemning, but I am truly not. I'm stating why the issue exists. At this point, I am no longer shocked at who secretly indulges in same-sex relationships.

We have reached an all-time high in the scandals coming out of the church. The secrets that lie within the church are truly sad.

Why so many secrets?

I used to ask myself this question. How is it possible for the church, the body of Jesus Christ, the bride of Christ, to do so many things behind closed doors? The answer lies within every human. The answer is worn every single day. It all has to do with the flesh. We are still human. Although we have the Lord and are anointed, we are still flesh and blood. We are still wrapped in flesh that originates from earth while trying to live a godly lifestyle. The flesh will always desire what is contrary to what the spirit wants.

Paul says this in his letter to the Galatians. He tells them that flesh is contrary to the spirit, and the spirit is contrary to the flesh. He goes on to say that they oppose each other. The ultimate goal of the flesh is to not allow you to do what you want, which is to serve the Lord. *For the flesh desires what is contrary to the Spirit, and the Spirit what is contrary to the flesh. They are in conflict with each other, so that you are not to do whatever you want" (Galatians 5:17 NIV).*

Once many reach a certain level in ministry, it is very hard to admit wrongdoing. I know this too well because I was in this situation. It takes a very strong-willed and deep-rooted person in God to be able to humble themselves, confess, and admit the sins they have committed. This is telling of the condition that the church finds itself in. So many things go on in many congregations that when they come out, they sound so scandalous.

It is all coming out!

As of late, there have been many reports of scandals coming out like never before from within the church of Jesus Christ. We have to remember that judgment starts in the church first. God's pattern of judgment is that he deals with his own people first. It is true with the nation of Israel as it still stands with the church today. God is starting to allow exposure within his church. Through it, he is cleaning his church of all that is wrong with it. God is not silent when it comes to sin. But rather, he is patient. He gives opportunities for repentance. But he is judging his house!

"For it is time for judgment to begin with God's household; and if it begins with us, what will the outcome be for those who do not obey the gospel of God?" (1 Peter 4:17 NIV).

Not too long ago, a scandal broke out involving the senior pastor of a prominent global church based out of Australia. The pastor resigned over misconduct with two females. These alleged incidents happened over a span of ten years. He was already dealing with criminal charges of concealing sexual abuse by his late father in the 1970s. Why now? Why would all this have to be dealt with after all this time? Well, simply because no one gets away with it. But the question is why does God want to deal with it?

Zechariah avenged

To know how God works, you have to look at the patterns of God and how he operated in the Bible. Zechariah was a prophet in ancient Israel. His name means "God remembers." Jesus accused and charged the Pharisees with the death of a prophet that died roughly around five-hundred-plus years BC. So why bring it up at that moment? Well, because Zechariah was murdered. He was murdered in between the door and altar of the temple on the Sabbath. This, that was done, was done in secret because Zechariah was preaching the truth to the religious that were in control. He was also one of them. They turned their backs on him. They conspired against him and killed him in secret, thinking that no one saw it.

Little did they know that God would take his very name into account in the matter. Jesus is now holding them accountable for his murder. You might say, "But they weren't the ones who killed him." But the mindset and the ideology was the same. Because of preaching truth, many conspired against Zechariah. Many labeled him and ostracized him, then murdered him in between the door and the altar behind closed doors, out of the view of the rest of people. But God saw it. God leaves no stone unturned. God deals with everything.

> My eyes are on all their ways; they are not
> hidden from me, nor is their sin concealed from
> my eyes. I will repay them double for their wick-
> edness and their sin, because they have defiled my
> land with the lifeless forms of their vile images
> and have filled my inheritance with their detest-
> able idols. (Jeremiah 16:17–18 NIV)

Abortion is nothing now

Sometime ago, I was given some news of a colleague in the ministry, about how he was diagnosed with cancer. I was so sad to hear this news. Upon hearing this devastating news, the Holy Spirit whispered to me and said, "He was not sincere." I was taken aback when I heard this. The Holy Spirit was telling me that the cancer was due to something the man did. I, of course, did some investigating and found that he knew of things his children were doing and never corrected them. The church members would confront him, and he would deny it. He would lash out at the church for attacking his family.

Things got so bad that his oldest daughter got pregnant, and instead of dealing with it, both him and his wife took her to get an abortion. This is truly devastating. This is not easy to deal with. God wants honesty. God wants transparency. The pastors, elders, and leaders are not above reproach. God deals with us equally. This is the cause of many people that are sick within the church of Jesus Christ. Confession brings healing.

Where have the power, miracles, signs, and wonders gone?

I have heard many people comment on how they no longer see the power, miracles, signs, and wonders like they used to long ago. In the times of Oral Roberts, Billy Graham, A. A. Allen, there used to be visual manifestations of the power of God with ease in camp meetings. Now is it true that there is no more power, miracles, signs, and wonders in our meetings? Well, the obvious answer is no, it's not true. Clearly God is still moving in our congregations, but there is something to be said about the frequency with which God moves today.

There has been a diminishing factor in the power, miracles, signs, and wonders in today's church. The question is not, "Is this happening?" but, rather, "Why is this happening?" The answer lies with the church. God can and still moves today, but when sin and unbelief is prevalent, the manifestation of the power of God is not. If you have studied the Bible, then you see a pattern on how God moves and operates. God tells Solomon that he will be present and heal the land on which they live. Sin is what stops God from being present and doing what he does best, bless his people.

"If my people, who are called by my name, will humble themselves and pray and seek my face and turn from their wicked ways, then I will hear from heaven, and I will forgive their sin and will heal their land" *(2 Chronicles 7:14 NIV).*

The glory of God has departed

This same issue happens in the book of Ezekiel. In the eighth chapter, the prophet is told by the Lord to look in the temple to see what was being done by the priests. As he looked, he saw how they were committing idolatry. They were defiling the holy temple of the Lord. The temple was where God and only God was to be worshipped. They were doing the complete opposite. They were committing all kinds of sin. In chapter 10, God later shows the prophet in a vision that he has removed his glory from the temple. It was sin that caused God to remove his glory from the temple.

It wasn't just any sin that caused God to remove his glory from the temple. It was hidden sin, sin that was done in secret. The one's that bore the responsibility of keeping the presence of God in the nation were the ones committing the very sins that would make God take his presence and glory away. The church needs to get honest and transparent. There has to be a cleansing of the ministerial body of Christ. No more backroom worldliness with a public holiness. No more oversexualized clothing on the altars.

No more singing worldly music and dressing it up with the name of Jesus. These things hinder the move of God in congregations. You may think it's legalism what I am saying, but the character and nature of God has never changed. We have to stop the secret sins and embrace clean living and the truth of God. The world should feel shame and conviction when they see the church of Jesus Christ. Instead, many times, they feel the sense of entitlement to be able to judge the church with how the church is living. Now please understand that I don't mean all in the church.

The church will always be the holy sanctified bride of Christ. But there are some that represent the church that give the church a bad name to many. So let's start holding ourselves accountable and step out of the shadows and into the light. God is the rewarder of truth and integrity.

10
Right Where I Left Off

A few years have passed since backsliding. The beckoning of the Holy Spirit was unbearable and inescapable. It was every day. He would tug on my heart while still in a relationship with the other female. I didn't know how to get out of it. I missed the presence of the Lord like never before. I missed being randomly touched by his love while just sitting on my sofa, watching television. I missed the times at night when I would pray, and he would whisper in my ear. I missed his fire.

Now here I am, parked in a Kmart parking lot, in my work truck. I'm crying my eyes out. I reached out to someone to pray for me because I just couldn't take it anymore. After so long, I was willing to let my guard down for someone to minister to me. But before I get into what happened next, I have to tell you how I got to this point. I have to walk you through the journey the Holy Spirit had me go through. It was a very emotionally tasking and draining experience, one I know that many are going through at this very moment but don't know how to make sense of it. I wrote this to help you.

Why run?

I left the church because of guilt and shame. I knew I was wrong. I knew what I was doing was sinful. I knew that, eventually, ministering in the condition that I was in was going to force God to expose me. I always say that when someone knows the Lord, they don't leave him. I can honestly say that I did not know the Lord the way I know him now, but because I did not know him, I decided to run away from him, rather than run to him.

Backsliding is a sign that someone has not come to the realization of who God is and who they are in him. We have to know our eternal position in Christ. God truly has made us sons and daughters through the sacrifice of his one and only Son, Jesus Christ. The apostle Paul tells us that the Spirit we have received brought about our adoption to sonship.

"The Spirit you received does not make you slaves, so that you live in fear again; rather, the Spirit you received brought about your adoption to sonship. And by him we cry, 'Abba, Father'" (Romans 8:15 NIV).

Those that know they are sons and daughters understand that they all have the confidence in the world to run to the Father in time of trouble. They recognize that, yes, the Father may be angry, but they also know that his anger lasts but for a moment. The anger of the Lord does not last for a long time. He has the right amount of anger and time to deal with us because he would rather spend more time loving us than chastising us.

"For his anger lasts only a moment, but his favor lasts a lifetime; weeping may stay for the night, but rejoicing comes in the morning" (Psalm 30:5 NIV).

Sons and daughters understand that although the Father is angry, they also know that he desires for us to be honest and go to him. When someone knows that they are in sonship, they are able to move about and approach the throne of grace with confidence because they know the desire of their Father is to have them close to him. Not knowing the concept of sonship will cause you to run from an angry god that desires to destroy you. But when you know and live in sonship, you run to God, even when you know you have fallen short of the glory of God.

Calloused and deactivated

I spent a considerable amount of time away from the Lord, three and a half years to be exact. I went from constantly being in the temple holding my Bible to holding a drink full of liquor. This was not who I truly was. I knew deep down inside I was a man of God. I was too afraid to come out of the shadows that I was so used to living in and into the light of Christ. Many have asked me how I could go from being in the presence of God one moment and the next moment be in a sinful lifestyle. The answer is easy. Continue to tell yourself that one little sin isn't a big deal or the famous "God understands."

Satan doesn't need you to do many sins in order to trap you. He just needs you to do one sin and do it repeatedly. Because once you do it repeatedly, your heart gets calloused. You become desensitized to the sin that you are doing. You become less and less fearful of the act of sin that it becomes easier to sin. Once your heart becomes calloused, you begin to disconnect your spirit from the Holy Spirit, causing deactivation. This is what happened to me. The addiction to porn got me to a calloused state in my heart and deactivated my spirit. My low and poor spiritual state opened the door for the devil and gave him the opportunity to tempt me with another woman. I took the bait.

The lion and its prey

Do you understand now? Do you see why I ran? I became good at running. I was so good at running that I ran into so many issues. God has his plans, but so does the devil. The devil and his cohorts have devised a plan for your life, just like God has. Part of their plan is to make you run away from the presence of God.

"Be alert and of sober mind. Your enemy the devil prowls around like a roaring lion looking for someone to devour" (1 Peter 5:8 NIV).

Satan and his cohorts attempt to convince people to leave from the world and life they always knew. In the mind of the enemy lives the same plan that lions have. Lions try to separate their prey from the rest of the pack. They will roar. With their roar, they instill fear in the pack. The ones that get consumed with fear will run off. The rest of the pack huddles together because they know that together, they are stronger than any lion. The one that flees is usually left alone.

Alone, they are an easy prey. This is what the enemy is doing to many. He is making many run away in fear. They are trying to make you run in fear of consequences, in fear of confrontation, and in fear of the work that it takes to repair the situation.

A father and his prodigal son

> The younger one said to his father, "Father, give me my share of the estate. So he divided his property between them." Not long after that, the younger son got together all he had, set off for a distant country and there squandered his wealth in wild living. (Luke 15:12–13 NIV)

Here we see that this father had two sons. The younger of the two asked for his inheritance and left to a far province. Why did he have to leave to a far-off province when he could have just stayed in his own city? Well, simply to be able to do the ungodly things he wanted to do, he had to go where no one knew him. The guilt and shame would have eaten him alive. This is what Satan does to so many people. He is convincing many people to leave and run far away, away from the presence of God. Oh, how thankful I am to God that he is a relentlessly pursuing God that does not quit.

I ran, he followed

I ran from God in hopes to escape the guilt, the shame, and the fallout of what was to be in my mind, the biggest scandal in my city and region. I began to do things I never saw myself doing. I was now in the very lifestyle that I used to preach against. I was now on the other side of grace and mercy. So I became the prodigal son. I ran away from my Father. Every night was so sad for me. I spent nights silently crying because I missed him, I missed the presence of my beloved. I could now understand the Shulammite woman that was after her beloved. The desperation she felt as she looked for him. My heart so longed for him like never before.

He would wake me up in the nighttime to speak to me. I would just turn around and just cry with shame. I knew I was not worthy of him. But that's how deep the enemy got in my mind and heart. He made me believe that God was done with me. He made me believe that there was no hope for me. The entire time I was running, unbeknownst to me, God was setting me up for my freedom. He was pursuing me with a relentless passion. His heart burned for me like Solomon for the Shulammite. God will seek after us and not mind the obstacles. We belong to him.

> For this is what the Sovereign Lord says: I myself will search for my sheep and look after them. As a shepherd looks after his scattered flock when he is with them, so will I look after my sheep. I will rescue them from all the places where they were scattered on a day of clouds and darkness. (Ezekiel 34:11–12 NIV)

God desires to set us free

Throughout the entire Bible, we can see the pattern of God, how he works and what he does for those that serve him. From Genesis to Revelation, we see how there is distress, siege, prison, and liberation. God always lifted up a liberator. He even speaks to the prophet Micah about the Spirit of the breaker, one that would come and break his people free from their bondage.

"The One who breaks open the way will go up before them; they will break through the gate and go out. Their King will pass through before them, the Lord at their head" (Micah 2:13 NIV).

God did not make us to be bound. He did not create us to be bogged down with sin and disease. He created us to be free in him. He gave us the power to be called the sons of God. That means that his design for us is to experience what it is to be a member of his household. In his house, everyone has the right to live in the life that he provides. He provides true freedom. He gives us his word to break free from things that roam around in the mind.

It was my turn

It was my turn to finally be free. In public, I showed how happy I was. But deep down, I was drowning in my misery. I was secretly desiring to be free of this adulterous relationship that I found myself in. What was stopping me was the fear of hurting her. You see, the enemy created a false reality that entrapped me. It didn't allow me to be free. This is something that the enemy does.

False reality

The enemy knows that preachers know the Word of God. So what he does is use the Word to trap the preacher. I was trapped with knowing that what I was living was a sin. I did not know how to come clean, but my soul was so tired of being away from God. I would wake up tired and go to sleep tired, tired of my sin. On the other side, the woman I was in this adulterous relationship also wanted to be free but didn't know how to be free as well. She also was trapped with the thought of hurting me. She was afraid to cause me pain. That's what the enemy planted in both our minds. He created a false reality to keep us trapped. That's all it is, false. The enemy is an expert at presenting false realities because he tells lies since the beginning.

But in this case, I was ready to come out of my grave. I could not stay in the relationship anymore. My wife was feeling all of the pain. She was feeling deserted. She was left alone to fend for herself. That is not what God called a man to do. He designed the man to be a provider, protector, and comforter for his helpmate. He is to be one with his wife. How can a man push his wife away from himself when he and his wife are one? I needed to allow God to heal my wife. God couldn't heal her until I came clean about my life.

Living a lie

Up until this point, I lived a lie. I could no longer keep up with the facade. I was so used to lying to hide who I was that I didn't know how to be real. I didn't know how to let my guard down enough to show people who I was because who I was, was someone I hated and despised. I was so embarrassed of who I was and where I came from that I had to lie. Boy, did I lie well. I was such a liar that I couldn't tell the truth no matter what I did. I lied, even when I had no reason to lie. I lied, even when the best thing to do was to tell the truth, and I would purposely lie because that was all I knew. This is the life of those that live in fear.

God wants us to live in the truth of his love. That truth is Jesus Christ. He is the way, the truth, and the life. He is the truth of the Father. When he is in someone's life, they have no reason to live in the darkness of deception. In fact, they cannot live in darkness. That goes against their new nature. By this time, God was breaking me from deep within. I was being bombarded with scripture and thoughts of freedom daily in my mind. God would push his desire for me to be free of everything that held me down and away from him.

The intensity and frequency with which God would minister to me was, at this point, unbearable. It was constant, and every single day. I would be with the woman I was in adultery with, and I would tell her I loved her because I didn't want to hurt her, but deep inside, I wanted to run to my wife and be happy. I wanted things to be the way God intended them to be. No one is designed to be bound. No human is created for a life in darkness. It was truly time for me to be set free. I had to get over the hurdle of fear. I had to get over the lies that the enemy was telling me. I needed a Spirit-filled, anointed minister of God to pray for me.

Everyone's connected

It would be foolish to believe that you're in this thing alone. The connection that is humanity is powerful. Everything came from one person. Eve came from Adam. Cain and Abel came from Adam and Eve. All of the people of the world came from them. We are all connected biologically and spiritually. Your freedom will eventually and ultimately result in someone else's freedom. God will free and save someone. Soon those around him will begin to experience the freedom that Christ provides. This was God's plan for my family and I. He wanted to bring us all back but needed to set one free first. This is why God is relentlessly pursuing you. He wants you to be free because there are so many that are connected to you. There are so many that need to come to Christ, and you are the person that God wants to use to set them free. He has called you to be the key to open the door to their prison cell. Through your obedience, many will be blessed. This is the promise God gave Abraham.

> I will surely bless you and make your descendants as numerous as the stars in the sky and as the sand on the seashore. Your descendants will take possession of the cities of their enemies, and through your offspring all nations on earth will be blessed, because you have obeyed me. (Genesis 22:17–18 NIV)

Chains have to break

It was a Friday afternoon, and I'm almost done with my work day. I got a job as a delivery driver. It was nearing the end of my route. But I just couldn't get the feeling out of my head and heart. Now I wasn't a stranger of visiting the church while I was backslidden. During the time I was out, I visited about three times. I remember one of the last times I visited, there was a guest speaker at the church. He was a true man of God. He preached his sermon. At the end of the preaching, he made an altar call. I did not want to go up, but I did. I went up, and he began to pray for me. God began to use him to speak to me. God began to tell me what was to come. It was so real.

I needed to be free! God was preparing my heart for the freedom of my soul. God doesn't just set someone free. This is why I encourage you to pray hard and don't give up for the person you're praying for to surrender to the Lord. There are things in the background that God is doing for them to be set free. God systematically will break down every barrier for them to be set free. Have patience,

God is working. Just as he does for everyone, he was doing the same to me. He was breaking chains in me, little by little. You see, at the time that I left the Lord, my parents also backslid. I was the strong one for my family. There is almost always one person that keeps the people together. That's usually what a shepherd does. That day, God used the preacher to speak to me about my parents and family.

A parking lot

Now here I am, parked in a Kmart parking lot, in my work truck. I'm crying my eyes out. I reached out to someone to pray for me because I just couldn't take it anymore. After so long, I was willing to let my guard down for someone to minister to me. I reached out to someone to point me to someone that was really used by the Lord. They gave me the phone number of a female prophetess of the Lord. I gave her a call, and little did I know, God was going to use her to speak to my life. I called her, and she answered. As I spoke to her, I began to tell her about my situation. She interrupted me and began to finish my story. God began to speak to me through her and tell me specific details. As she spoke to me, she told me what my sin was. She was able to tell me what I did and who I did it with. But then, she said something that truly set me free of the fear, she told me that God truly loved me, and he was not angry. We often have this image of an angry God, but what we fail to understand, sometimes, is that God is love. He desires to love us. His forgiveness, grace, and mercy is so great.

We will never understand how great and how wide is his love for us. In fact, the Bible says that God throws our sins in the sea. Now, of course, it is not the literal sea that he throws our sins in. But he forgets about them.

"You will again have compassion on us; you will tread our sins underfoot and hurl all our iniquities into the depths of the sea" (Micah 7:19 NIV).

This is what the religious will never understand. We not only are forgiven, but God also does not bring up our sins to us once he forgives us. It is truly just as he says in the Word. It's as if he throws them into the sea. Can you find anything in the sea once it falls in? Can you see when you look into the sea? This is what God does. He remembers them no more. I thank God for his love and forgiveness.

Right where I left off

I repented that day. I rededicated my life to Christ. I gave my heart to him again. I was immediately inundated with waves of love and forgiveness. I couldn't take it. I was on my knees in that parking lot and did not care who saw me. The passersby looked at me. But I could not stop saying how sorry I was to the Lord. I could not stop saying, "Thank you, Jesus." I was overwhelmed with the presence of God. I thought I would never feel that again.

Once I got home, I messaged my pastor. I told him what I did. It was such a long time that I did not speak to him. He told me that he was happy to hear me and that God was pleased. I felt like a brand-new man. I felt like I was just born again. I told him I wanted to publicly give my heart to the Lord at the altar. I felt it was important because up until that time, I was living recklessly publicly. So I saw it fit to give that up publicly.

As soon as I got back to the Lord, I started to feel his direction again. God began to move in my life like never before. He began to minister to me more clearly. He began to speak to my heart so powerfully. I was now in a new relationship with him. Almost a year into my walk with him again, he began to put in my heart to leave my job. Things were going right where I left off. Things were headed back to how they were at the time when I backslid. It was as if God was saying, "You stopped and got off my plan, now get back on it." God knows what he is doing, and his gift and calling is irrevocable. He does not throw away his original plan for you. When you come out of darkness, he picks up with you right where you left off.

"For God's gifts and his call are irrevocable" (Romans 11:29 NIV).

God is not angry

This is so freeing. This is what keeps so many away from going back to the Lord. This is what keeps so many people in darkness. God is not angry with you! He wants to forgive you. I lived in fear. I lived in fear in church, I lived in fear wherever I was. I looked at life and God through the lens of control. I was so used to hearing sermons of fear. Any little sin was going to get God to reveal your sin and hurt you some way. To me, God was so angry at all times. He was angry only with those that had to listen to the sermon, but not with the one who preached it. I didn't know any better. I didn't know any better because I was a lazy Christian. I didn't read the Word for myself. I read just enough to satisfy my religious duty and responsibility, but I didn't get deep enough to truly know the truth. Yes, God gets angry and hates sin, but he desires to have mercy. He desires for us to live holy and righteous lives. He wants to love us. My friend, brother, sister, God is not angry with you. He loves you and wants you to be free. He inspired me to write this book to pull you out of that dark place. Jesus loves you!

11

It Is for Freedom

The apostle Paul testifies to the church members in Galatia that he received the revelation of the mystery of the Gospel of Jesus Christ by Jesus Christ himself. He did not receive it by man nor was he taught it. It was by revelation of God himself. Paul is reaching out to them and tries to bring them back from the bondage that they were placing themselves in again with leaving the freedom that came from the grace of Jesus Christ for the legalism of the Judaizers.

They were being fooled, according to Paul. They were leaving the freedom of uncircumcision for circumcision. In doing so, they would have to obey the law, rather than the grace of Jesus Christ. This is such a travesty. Paul was dumbfounded. He was so perplexed as to who bewitched them to leave the faith that was revealed to them. This is how some of us feel when we see someone leave the grace and their walk with the Lord Jesus Christ.

Sometimes it is so hard to understand, but this comes down to knowing the foundation on which you stand on. Not knowing where you stand means you don't know where you are. Not knowing where you are means you don't know where you are going. Not knowing where you are going means you don't know who sent you and what your mission is. Sadly enough, there are many Christians and ministers in this very predicament. Many preachers preach but do not understand why they have to preach.

I don't say this just to say it. I say it because I lived it. I preached and did not have a clear understanding of my calling, my mission, and the vision. I could not see the end goal for what I was doing. I was simply doing because that's what I was told I had to do. I preached without feeling the weight of the calling. I preached without feeling the responsibility. I preached without feeling the love for the souls I preached to. It was a show. It was me chasing what I thought was ministerial success.

Why do this?

A preacher needs to know why he or she has to preach or else they will only be doing what is socially accepted, rather than what is heavenly expected. So why preach? When the power of the Holy Spirit touches someone that has been bound, they usually begin to tell everyone about their experience. Let's look at why this happens. We have to preach the Gospel because it is freedom that cannot be contained reaching the soul. It is ever-flowing power that, like electricity, has to find a way out.

Grace

When the grace of Jesus Christ reaches us, it comes as a rushing wave, a tidal wave, and tsunami, even. His love overwhelms us, and there's no way to contain the joy and happiness one feels. The apostle John says that out of God's fullness, we received grace upon grace.

"Out of his fullness we have all received grace in place of grace already given" (John 1:16 NIV).

His fullness is everything that he is. He holds nothing back. He gives you all of himself. Grace does not stay stagnant nor does it just stay in one place. This is why when you see someone come to Christ, they start to tell everyone. When the grace of Jesus touches us, it makes us free, and free people want to make others free. This is why you see people preach immediately. I know, at times, it can be annoying with how insistent they are. Sometimes judgmental, even.

But think about why they do this. They were just set free from the grasps of the enemy. They were once held down by the kingdom of darkness. They have been set free and now live in the light of freedom. They want to tell everyone what made them free. That's what grace does. Grace screams from the rooftops! Someone will hear grace's voice. That voice is the voice of Jesus through yours.

Anointing

In that same manner, the anointing of the Holy Spirit breaks the yoke of bondage that holds someone down. It destroys the chains that keep someone captive to their destructive lifestyle. One of the purposes of the anointing is to break the yoke. First you have to understand what a yoke is. A yoke is a wooden crosspiece that is fastened over the necks of two animals and attached to the plow or cart that they are to pull. The yoke is how the farmer can control the animal to work for him. It is how the farmer gets animals to do his bidding.

Satan is lazy. He cannot work for himself. He can only do evil in this world when there is someone to do what he makes them do, through the power of mental control and suggestion. How can he so easily do this? He can do this when the thoughts of a person are not guarded. He can control people with the yoke that he places on their minds. Like an animal, you will begin to do the works of darkness because there is a yoke on your neck. The anointing breaks that yoke to set you free.

A wild freedom

Imagine a fox that was caught in a bear trap. The pain it feels because of the trap. The despair that runs through its mind. Imagine now that a human comes and takes the fox, opens the bear trap, and sets it free. Almost always, the fox will run away, but it runs wild. Why so wild? Well, simply because it was free before it got caught in the trap. That is how we are. We were never made to be bound. We were created to be in freedom. When Jesus comes and breaks the yoke and takes the trap off us, we experience wild freedom. Now imagine all that I just told you. Do you not see why people begin to preach? This is why we must preach the Gospel. Remember this: free people free people!

> You, my brothers and sisters, were called to be free. But do not use your freedom to indulge the flesh; rather, serve one another humbly in love. For the entire law is fulfilled in keeping this one command: "Love your neighbor as yourself." (Galatians 5:13–14 NIV)

It was time to end it

Now as I got deeper and closer to the Lord, I knew that there was one major hurdle I had to jump. It was the one thing that was stopping me from truly seeing all that grace had to offer. It was the adulterous relationship I had with the other woman. I'm sure some of you are thinking, *Why didn't you let that go right away? That's what I would have done.* What many people don't understand is that God walks us through our deliverance. He walks with us with patience.

There are some chains that break immediately, and there are some chains that break over time. God knows what to do to get you free and how to get you free. He was defeating the spirit of fear in me. Not only was I learning to have to defeat fear, but I also had to defeat lust and perversion. These spirits work together. If I would have just broken off the relationship, the enemy would have another female ready for me to fall with.

I said before, sanctification is a process. Sometimes, it takes time. But the good news is that it happens. The apostle Paul says it like this, *"Being confident of this, that he who began a good work in you will carry it on to completion until the day of Christ Jesus" (Philippians 1:6 NIV).*

Sometimes, you can't care

There was such a fear in me. I didn't want to hurt this woman. I didn't want her to leave the Lord because of me. I was so afraid of being exposed and to have so many people potentially leave the Lord because of it that I just stayed in my sin. I was so afraid to tell her that it was over. The freedom was now in my heart, but the courage to let go was not. I was engulfed in the deception of the enemy. He didn't want to let us go. He wanted to keep me trapped and keep her trapped. As heartless as this sounds, you can't care sometimes. No matter what they will feel, you just have to sever all ties or else you'll be trapped and ultimately destroyed.

This is a tactic that has proven to be a very affective and effective one for the enemy as he uses it against men and women of God, to trap them in sin. Just as the Lord tugs at the heart, so does he. The enemy uses feelings and emotions to keep us trapped. This is why the Word of God says in Proverbs, *"Above all else, guard your heart, for everything you do flows from it" (Proverbs 4:23 NIV).*

Ishmael has to go

I spoke about Abraham in chapter 2. But I would like to speak about him once more as this is crucial for my point here. If he can get you to invest yourself into something, then he can get you to wrestle with letting it go. This same thing happened to Abraham. God promised him that he would have a child with his wife, Sarah. At the time, their names were Abram and Sarai. They had a few things going against them: their age (about seventy-five), and his wife was barren. But God insisted that they would have a child. Time passed by. In fact, twenty-five years would pass before they would see the promise fulfilled.

It was so much that Sarai got the brilliant idea to help God. Does this sound familiar? Has this been you in your walk with God? Sometimes, we get desperate in waiting for the promise that we tend to stick our hands in the situation. God told them that he would give them a child. But instead, she forgot the word spoken to them and looked at her situation. She had an Egyptian slave named Hagar. She convinced Abram to lay with Hagar to have a son. This was a plan from none other than Satan himself. God gave a promise. He did not need any help to do what he promised.

If you know theology, it is widely accepted that Egypt represents the world. The promise of God would not need the world's assistance. God does not need human help. It was so much that he had a son with Hagar. They named him Ishmael. Ishmael was not a part of the promise of God for Abram and Sarai. But the child grew up with Abram and Sarai. In fact, he came from Abram. Abram loved his son, Ishmael. He was a part of his heart.

Ishmael will mess with your Isaac

God now is faithful to his promise made to Abram. Sarai is now pregnant with the promised child. She gives birth to a son. They name him Isaac. Isaac is truly the son of the promise that God made Abram. Now Abram, instead of having one son, as originally intended by God, has two sons. They grow together. They are half brothers but brothers nonetheless. One day, Sarai (whose name is now Sarah) sees that the son of the Egyptian was mocking her son, Isaac. She said to her husband (whose name is now Abraham) to get rid of Hagar and her son, Ishmael. The Bible says that the matter distressed Abraham so much because it involved his son.

> The child grew and was weaned, and on the day Isaac was weaned Abraham held a great feast. But Sarah saw that the son whom Hagar the Egyptian had borne to Abraham was mocking, and she said to Abraham, "Get rid of that slave woman and her son, for that woman's son will never share in the inheritance with my son Isaac." The matter distressed Abraham greatly because it concerned his son. (Genesis 21:8–11 NIV).

It was important for him to let him go. What he did not see at the moment was the danger that Ishmael's presence was posing, just by being there. Since Ishmael was the firstborn, the inheritance would have legally gone to him, instead of Isaac. The Ishmael in you, the thing or person you were never called to is messing with your purpose. It's mocking your calling. It's attempting to steal your inheritance. The longer it stays in your heart, the longer it has to claim legal right to you. As horrible as it sounds, Sarah was right. Ishmael had to go. You need to do the same. Your Ishmael has to go. I had to let her go.

God will show you why

With Abraham being so distressed, it is clear that he struggled with this decision. It was difficult and painful for him because Ishmael was a part of him. This is what is happening to many preachers that are living this situation. Many preachers and Christians alike are living double lives. It is very hard for them to let go of the other person they're with or the porn addiction or whatever vice they have controlling their lives. But having an understanding of why you must let go helps so much.

God had to help Abraham make the decision. God had to assist Abraham because, otherwise, Abraham would not let him go. The pain it caused Abraham, I'm sure was great. I'm sure it must have felt like a piece of his heart was being ripped apart. But it was necessary. This was also happening to me. I spent a long time in this adulterous relationship with this other woman. It felt like she was a part of me and I of her.

But I had to let her go. Having her in my life wouldn't have just destroyed me, but it would have destroyed her as well. I wasn't the only one that God called to do his will. She was also called to work for the Lord. God had to speak to me and assist me in the decision, just like he did to Abraham.

"But God said to him, 'Do not be so distressed about the boy and your slave woman. Listen to whatever Sarah tells you, because it is through Isaac that your offspring will be reckoned'" (Genesis 21:12 NIV).

God is so full of grace toward us that even knowing that we stepped into something that can and will potentially destroy us will continue to fight for us and help us out of our mess. His Holy Spirit does not rest. He continues to speak to us and remind us of his promises for us. He spoke to me day and night about it.

The day came

I remember waking up one morning, feeling the presence of God. I woke up knowing that I had to end it. Now her and I would try to break it off from time to time. We broke it off for quite some time, up until this particular morning. The issue was that we would break it off but would not truly do it from the heart. We always left a back door open. We always went as far as our hearts allowed us. There were days and weeks that would go by without us speaking to each other. But as soon as that demonic spirit would come, he would put a thought in our heads or hearts, and we would contact each other once again. Thus starting the vicious cycle.

But on this particular day, God wanted for us to truly be set free. I remember her contacting me as we spent about almost a whole month without speaking to each other. What's wild about all this is that I had a feeling that she would be calling. That day, she did just as I felt. When I heard her voice, I felt the nervousness once again. I knew that if I fell back into it with her, I most likely wouldn't be able to get out.

As I answered, I could hear the pain in her voice. I could hear the despair. I could feel my flesh wanting her again. While this is happening, I also heard the voice of the Holy Spirit speaking to me. I could feel my spirit telling me to run. I could feel the Spirit of God saying, "Hang up!" As I spoke to her, I felt myself almost returning to the old mindset. I remember the Holy Spirit saying, "We have too much to lose." When I heard that, I knew that it was time to end it. I finally felt the weight of the calling. I finally felt the responsibility of ministry. I finally loved the people I preached to. I truly felt fear, but it wasn't a fear that came from the enemy.

This fear came from my love for the Lord. I felt what Joseph felt when Potiphar's wife was telling him to sleep with her. He felt fear. The fear he felt was the fear he had to fall short before the Lord. I never felt this before. I never felt this type of fear, the fear that one feels when they know they could lose too much, when they know they could lose it all. I had a good thing going with the Lord and my wife. My wife was starting to get healed. God was restoring our marriage. He was finally doing the things that he promised to do. Now I was at a crossroads. I was faced with the decision that could either make or break me.

I told her that it was truly time to let it go and end this relationship once and for all. I told her that we could not do this any longer. I told her that that was the last time her and I would speak. She did what I knew she would do: cry. I cried as well. I told her that I knew that God wanted for us both to be free. Trust me, hearing the breaking of a heart is hard enough, but to know that the heart that is breaking is breaking because of you is on a whole other level. This was one of the hardest things I ever had to do. But, boy, am I glad I did it. I was set free that day.

God truly did it. He gave me the courage to break what I once thought was impossible to break. His love for me was great. The amount of patience he displayed through all of that was just amazing. Not only did he break that relationship, but he also broke me free from the addiction to porn that day. He broke me free from the hold lust had on me. I can say that since that day, I have not struggled with pornography and lust like I did then. Of course, the urge and temptation never truly leave us, but it is now like any other temptation.

Coming clean wasn't as clean

I now had to come clean to my wife. This to me was the hardest thing I have ever had to do. She would ask me what happened with me and the other woman. If I ever did anything with her. If I actually had sex with her. I lied to her for years. I lied to her about what truly happened between the other woman and I. I lied because I was afraid that she would leave me. I lied because I thought that it would be the biggest scandal.

But that also was a lie of the enemy. Coming clean and confessing is what I needed to bring everything out of the dark and into the light. If it can be in darkness, it can hide and stay. But if light is shed on it, it has no place to hide and has to go. Coming clean and confessing breaks the curse in your lineage. It releases you of past curses that live and travel through your bloodline. Like I said in previous chapters, confessions brings healing. This is how we heal. Not just spiritually but physically.

There was an atmosphere of grace

For an entire month, my wife was after me about telling her the truth. She said what wives typically say, "I know you did it. I just want to hear it." I kept saying I did nothing, and that it was only emotional cheating. I did not dare tell her I actually had a sexual relationship with the other woman. But what she said next really ministered to me. It actually gave me the courage to open up and confess. She said to me, "No matter what you tell me, God's grace is powerful enough to get us through this."

That opened my heart. I felt safe to speak because my words were going to be met with grace. I felt okay in knowing that even if she decided to get a divorce, things were going to be okay because God's grace was powerful enough to get us through it, no matter the outcome.

I paused for a second. I began to confess it all. I cannot tell you how free it made me feel. We both cried for hours and hours that Saturday. God did it. He finally brought me out of the dark and into the light. It was as if I could see for the first time. I felt like I could breathe without any issue or trouble. It felt as if I was in the deepness of the ocean, trying to reach the surface with little to no oxygen left in my lungs and finally breaching the surface. I was free! I was in the light of the Lord.

Preacher, brother, sister, and fellow believer, I pray that upon reading this book, you find the freedom you so desperately need. I pray that you break free of what has you bound. I pray that the Holy Spirit of God shines his glorious light on you and shows you all that is in your heart because then and only then will you be able to clean up the mess. Today is the day of freedom for you. I pray that you step out of the darkness and into the light!

"It is for freedom that Christ has set us free. Stand firm, then, and do not let yourselves be burdened again by a yoke of slavery" (Galatians 5:1 NIV).

About the Author

Michael Quiñones is the lead pastor and founder of Christ Saves Church in Lancaster, Pennsylvania. Alongside his wife, Elizabeth, they serve their community. Michael was born and raised in the city of Lancaster, Pennsylvania. Early in his life, he was drawn to leaning to play music to escape his harsh reality and upbringing. Michael became a worship leader in his church. Soon after, he studied theology at El Shaddai Biblical Institute.

After graduating, he began to teach at the institute. He began his evangelistic ministry, traveled, preaching the Word of God all over the United States and abroad from 2003 until 2020, when he founded Christ Saves Church.